SMALL CITY
BIG PAPER

by A-TOWN

RoseDog Books

PITTSBURGH, PENNSYLVANIA 15238

RoseDog Books
585 Alpha Drive
Suite 103
Pittsburgh, PA 15238
Visit our website at www.rosedogbookstore.com

ISBN: 978-1-4809-7886-7
eISBN: 978-1-4809-7909-3

WHEN a person mentions places where niggas are getting real money, you never hear South Carolina in the conversation, let alone Orangeburg. The south has been overlooked so long as a place to get money up until the last 20 years or so, Atlanta and Miami has put a spin on that notion. People have started to recognize the south for what it is. It's a hot spot for getting money and nice weather to splurge the money. In this book, we are not talking about states such as GA, Texas, Florida or so. No, this book will be talking about South Carolina. Then I want to know what you know about the Dirty South!! Many rappers from all over have gave little shot outs about South Carolina but none tell the truth about SC or they may not even know the truth. We get and spend BIG PAPER down here. The real get money niggas know how us South Carolina niggas get down. We get down for that paper. We do some major numbers to say that we are small. Some even call us country but these country boys know how to get paper. Orangeburg is the city we are talking about, gets real paper, real money. We do Big Boy shit and have Big Boy toys down here. I'm talking about 745's, S 430's, S 550's, Range Rover's,650's, Cadillac trucks, Lexus trucks, Infiniti trucks, even Maserati and Bentley GT's. I'm talking about paying all cash for these whips. No payments or credit. I'm talking about the feds coming in and digging up million dollars from under a pool. Niggas getting pulled over with 75 stacks cash and just tell the police they can have that! Nigga get hit with 60 grand cash in a hotel room and sign it over to the police. I don't want to tell you how many of them thangs get moved thru Orangeburg. I feel like how Pimp C said, "I would tell you cocaine numbers but you would think I was lying." We got P.S.I., DEA reports, FBI reports, IRS reports to back up this story. Niggas in the feds say they do this and they do that but you look at their PSI and they been working with a Big 8 at the most but they been getting money thou. LOL Really, they were just in the way…

PROLOGUE

As Ali lays in his bunk in Bennettsville Federal Correctional Institute he reflects on his life and what landed him there. His cell mate Top from Dillion SC who is another inmate with federal drug conspiracy charges ask Ali a question that gets him to think. "Ali, do you think that it was worth it to do what you did?". Ali really ponders over that question. He looks at the wall of pictures he has of all his kids and the different awards that they have achieved, he looks at all the pictures of all the many different countries, cities and places that he has visited over the years, he looks at the pictures of a lot of the females he has dealt with over the years, he looks at all the pictures of the cars and houses that he had. He shakes his head and smiles at all that he has done and seen. Then Ali thinks about what led him to get a federal sentence.........

Chapter 1
Get Rich or Die Trying

Ridgeland Correctional Institution
June 2002

"Yo Ali" Big Meat says

"What up my nigga" Ali Answers

"You about to get out soon, what you going to do when you hit them streets?" Big Meat asks. Ali really did not have to think of what to say because that's all he has been thinking about since he got locked up for violation last year.

"I'm about to get out and get that paper, next time you see me I will be a millionaire or I will be back in here with you with a life sentence" Ali says seriously. If 50 Cents album would have been out he would have said "Get Rich or Die Trying".

"I got like 8 more calendars to do and you know a nigga fucked up for real, fuck with your boy" Big Meats says. "My nigga, you know that I got you" Ali hits back. "I'm going to hook you up with Sauvé so you can get the pack and get your hustle on back here". They pound each up and say that's what it is. Ali hears his name on the loud speaker for visitation. Ali heads out the unit to the visitation hall. On the way, he is still thinking about how he will be getting out in about 3 months and try to do his thing in the streets. Ali walks thru the visitation door and spots his boo Rashawn at the far back table. He walks over and they hug and kiss and Ali gets to feel that fat ass of hers. "Boy, you better stop before we get in trouble" Rashawn tells Ali. They sit down and begin to converse. "You put that thing down where them people can get it?"

"Yep, I put it where I always put it" Rashawn reply.

"Damn Boo, Thank You". Since Ali has been doing time on this bid Rashawn has been making sure that Ali was straight and living comfortable. Rashawn has been dropping off the weed pack like clockwork every week so Ali's people can get it and bring it in to him.

"You don't have to thank me, I told you that I am a ride or die bitch" Rashawn says and looks at Ali directly in the eye.

"You been holding me down this whole bid so you know when I touch-down I'm going to hold you down for life" Ali holds her hand and said.

"Don't do that Ali, I do whatever I do because I love you, don't say that you going to be with me for that, I want you to be with me because you love me nothing else" Rashawn tell him seriously.

"You know that I love you for you but you just go the extra mile for a nigga" Ali spits

"By the way, what you want me to do with all the money that you are send-ing home?" she asks

"Boo it's your money so do what you want to do with it, you the one mak-ing this happen". They kick it for the rest of the visit and talk about what was going on in the city.

When Ali gets back to the unit his unit he stops by Suave cell and lets him know that the 'trees' are in place and the party should start tonight. Suave is an older cat from the Burg who was getting paper on the streets before he got knock. Ali likes to talk to the niggas before him in the game and try to get as much knowledge as he can and pointers on what to do and what not to do in the game.

"Lil nigga you don't play, do you?" Sauvé asks

"Nah, I'm about my business" Suave pulls out two streets size blunts and hands one to Ali and tell him to fire it up.

"Nigga you know I'm short, I ain't trying to catch no dirty urine"

"I got you, don't worry about that, I got the pills and you going to stay on that water, I ain't gonna let you go down". Ali says fuck it and lit up and they got zoned. While they were smoking Suave took the time to drop some jewels on Ali. "If you get out and hustle, do it for a reason"

"What you mean by that"

"I mean, go out and do things with that money, go places, see other parts of the world, don't just be no local baller or hustler and only think local". Ali thinks about what Suave is telling him.

"Enjoy that money" Suave speaks again and pulls out the photo albums. Ali looks at pictures of Suave in different places all over the world. Bahamas, Jamaica, Mexico, Cayman Island and more. Being high only intensifies how Ali looks at the pictures. Ali knows right then and there, that's what he wants to be and what he wants to do when he gets out. Ali have heard a lot of niggas say this and that and they did this and did that but it's true, A picture says a 1000 words. Ali looks at all the pretty water and pretty women, that's the good life he says to himself.

"That's what I'm trying to do when I get out" Ali tells Suave. Suave lets Ali know that he will be getting out in about a year and that he will make sure that his girl book them a trip somewhere exotic.

SEPT.2002

"You know that I max out in about 2 weeks" Ali tells the home team while they were having a smoke session. He lets them know that he going to have a baller bash for the homies before he leaves. They put the plan together and did it big the Saturday before Ali maxed out.

The day Ali maxed out him and Suave kicked it and Ali lets Suave know that he going to hold him down on getting the good weed in while he still doing his time. Suave always had the way to get the weed in but Ali knew where to get the good weed from.

"Take it lightly when you get out because it's easy to slip up and fall back in here" Sauvé tells Ali

"I ain't trying to come back but I ain't going to be broke either, I'm going to get that paper for real"

"Just be easy" Suave tells Ali as he walks out to go to the administration building. As Ali is walking all he can think about is how he going to get money. Whatever way he uses he must use them now because it's Show Time. While at Ridgeland Ali read a book called "True to da game" by Terri Woods, he could only think about how he wants to get money like that nigga "Q" in the book. It's going to be hard not being in a big city like in the book but Ali plans to do it big. After he reaches Admin he signs his release papers and the gun act.

CHAPTER 2
"STARTING FRESH"

"Hey Boo, what's going on with you" Ali ask over the phone.

"Waiting on you to call me and tell me to come and pick you up" Rashawn says.

"Girl I'm ready now, I done signed my release papers and waiting on you, I told you to be here at 8 o'clock" he says getting pissed off.

"Boy stop tripping, I'm outside" Rashawn laughs. Ali smiles and heads out the front door. As he walks outside he smells the fresh air and fresh scent of freedom. Ali looks up and say a silent thank you to God for getting him thru that hell on earth. He immediately sees Rashawn as she steps out of the car with a black and red Baby Phat outfit on with some black and red retro Jordan 11 to match. Ali walks to her and they embrace with a deep hug and kiss. Ali ask her to turn around so he can see how she looks. As she turns around he can see why Baby Phat makes so much money. Their clothes fit black women in all the right places and hug all the curves. "Let's go before I catch me a charge out here" Ali says with a devilish grin. When they got in the car Rashawn says, "I got a surprise for you".

"I know, I have been waiting almost two years for that" Ali said.

"I'm talking about something else boy" Rashawn says as she playfully hits him on the arm.

"What kind of surprise"

"Look on the back seat" Ali turns around and see bags from Lims, Macy's, Demos, Hibbets Sports and Foot Action. Ali goes thru the bags and find out he has Sean Jean, Roca wear, Akademics, and Ecko outfits along with all white and all black Air Force Ones and some of the same retro Jordan's that Rashawn has on. He knows that he is on point and let her know that she knows how to dress a nigga for real.

"You know your niggas off Dash Street done been calling me all day"

"What they talking about"

"They want to make sure I bring you thru the block as soon as we hit the Burg"(Burg is the term they call Orangeburg for short.)

"Damn, that can wait until tonight, I'm trying to layup"

"Well I done promise them that I was going to bring you thru there and besides you not going anywhere tonight, you have some making up to do." Rashawn smiles and tells him.

They drive the 2 ½ hours from the prison to the city and Ali thinks of what lies ahead of him. While he was incarcerated he heard his partner C-lo had Dash St. booming and money was coming thru. C-lo ended up getting knock and got sentenced to YOA just the month before. "Damn, I wish my dawg was out" Ali thinks to himself. 'We get that money together but I guess I have to get this paper by myself.' When they pull up on the block the Dash Street Crew that was home was all out there. Chin, Lo-Lo, The Thomas brothers, and Buck Wheat. Ali jumps out the car and yell "What ya'll thought ya'll wasn't going to see me" He walks up to the porch of one of the houses that they were trapping out of. A few of the homies give him a few dollars and ask him do he want to hit the dirty. (Dirty is weed laced with cocaine) Ali declines but grabs a Bud Light out of the cooler. He gets the run down on what's going on the block. He finds out that the block is dead and money is not coming thru like that no more. Damn a monkey wrench, well one monkey don't stop no show' he thinks.

Chin one of C-lo brothers asks, "So where you going"

"Well my girl got a room so I'm tied up tonight".

"Alright, come thru tomorrow so we can get this block back jumping" Chin tells him. The Dash Street crew knows that Ali knows how to get that paper. Ali pounds them up and heads to the hotel.

On the way to the room Ali knocks down the double deuce (22oz) Bud Light and starts to feel it. He looks over at Rashawn and see the Baby Phat jeans hugging her thighs and instantly his manhood rises to attention, "You need to hurry up and get to the hotel before I catch blue balls over here" he tells her. They pull up to the Howard Johnson on 601 and head to their room upstairs. As soon as the door closes they began to undress each other. Ali picks Rashawn up and throws her on the king size bed, he starts to kiss her all over and at the same time lets his fingers and hands rub all over her body. He takes one of her breast into his mouth and sucks on it as if he was a baby getting breast fed while caressing the other breast with his hand. All the while Rashawn is making hissing noises and whimpering in a low voice, Ali switches breast in his mouth and then moves his hands down between her legs. He notices now that her legs are moving involuntary open and close. Ali rubs down her clit in a few circular motions and then moves to her hole which is now dripping wet and inserts a finger. Her legs clamp tightly onto his hands as he slowly moves his finger in a back and forth motion. Ali moves his head up and starts to tongue kiss Rashawn and then feels the legs tight around his hand start to vibrate a little so he stop moving his finger and her body uncontrollably starts moving up and down on his finger. "I can't take this this no more, go ahead and put it in, I have been waiting months for this." Rashawn whispers between kisses, Ali grabs his rock-hard dick and rubs it on Rashawn soaked wet love box and then slips it in easily because she is so wet. She hisses as it goes in and open her legs wide so that her boo can do his thing. And that's what Ali did for about 30-45 minutes, even though he was locked up for about 18 months it wasn't no premature ejaculation going on.

After they finish they lay back on the bed with the tv turned on Court TV. That's one of Ali favorite stations to because he says it teaches you how other people fucked up and you think to do it different and it show you how to get away with murder. Which he knows he will need in his chosen profession. He thinks of ways to get the block back jumping. He asks Rashawn how much money do they have. And she lets him know that they only have $300. She then asks Ali is he mad at her. He thinks damn another monkey wrench but tells her no. He becomes quiet for a minute which makes Rashawn come to tears and say "you are mad at me and you over there acting anti-social like you do when you mad"

"I ain't mad!"

"Then why you looking like that". Ali thinks quick and says "I'm looking like this because I want some more good loving and you act like you tired". Rashawn smiles and say "I thought that you can't hang". With that she grabs Ali semi hard dick and gets it to turn brick hard with just a few soft strokes and then straddles him and begins to ride him like a champ. That was round two but that night they had about 4 rounds all together. Ali sat back after fucking her to sleep and thought about he only had about $700 to his name and how he would come up off that. Ali thinks he must call his God brother Sidney in the morning.

Early the next morning Ali sends Rashawn to the super Walmart to get him some boxer shorts and wife beaters. While she was gone, he called Sidney and got him to meet him up at the room. After he got there, they talked about a lot of things but what Ali wanted to really talk about was some dope and how to get some fast money

"shit is fucked up, my people up top is on E right now" Sidney says

"We got to come up with something because this being broke shit is not me" Ali tells him.

"Yeah, we got to put some shit together"

They kick it for a lil while more then Sidney lets him know that he will get him something to hold him over until they can see better days. After Sidney leaves Ali sits back and think about how he is back at square one. He looks over at Rashawn and thinks at least he has some good pussy to lay up in, so all is not lost. So, he decides to go for another round.

Chapter 3
"I'm All In"

Ali asks Rashawn to take him to Page Tec so that he can get a cell phone. The phone sets him back $200 but Ali knows that he is going to need communication when things get to jumping so he sees that as a good investment. After getting the cell phone, he heads to the East End barbershop on the boulevard to get a fresh line up, while over there he runs into a few niggas that he used to serve before he got locked up. He gives them his new cell number and lets them know he will be back in business soon so they can hit him up when they need to get straight. As he walks out of the barbershop he spots Jet, which is one of C-lo brothers that is getting money. Jet yell out the window "When you got out nigga"

"I just touchdown yesterday"

"You don't fuck with your boy no more"

"What's up". Jet tells Ali to jump in because they are holding up traffic. Ali tells Rashawn that he is going to ride with Jet and he will get up with her later. So, he bounces in the car with Jet in Jet's girl Honda. While riding, Ali gets down to the business of asking what is up. Jet lets him know that Sprinkle Ave is booming as always. "We always getting money on my block" Jet lets him know. Ali asks about the spot on Aaron street. Before Ali got locked up he use to hustle some dope for Jet at that spot. Jet goes on to tell Ali that after he got locked up that the crew that he had hustling for him at the spot started wilding out and serving any and everybody. "My nigga, the sled kicked in the door about 5 times so I shut that shit down." That's when Ali learns how C-Lo caught that secret indictment.

9

"Well I'm trying to crank Dash Street back up" Ali tells Jet.

"So, what you trying to get down with over there?"

"Shit, I'm going to move hard and soft" (hard is crack and soft is coke).

"You can come on Sprinkle and sell for me"

"Hell naw Jet, I am not fucking with you, you don't like to pay a nigga, let me get a half of ounce"

"How much money you got"

"About $350"

"My half goes for $500"

"Damn, nigga I'm just getting out"

"I will see what I can do." On the way over there, Ali thinks about the crack that Jet sells. It's some fire ass dope and the smokers love it. The only thing is Jet be taxing and dragging a nigga. He thinks to himself that Jet must be sitting on a mil ticket the way he drags niggas. He sells grams for $50 and you might not even get the whole gram and he don't sell no weight over a slab. (slab is a $100 worth of crack). When they got on Sprinkle the scene played out just as Ali thought it would. Jet tried to sell him 4 small slabs for the $350. Ali turns it down and calls one of the Dash Street boys to come and get him. While waiting on his ride he sees that Sprinkle Ave is getting some money by all the heavy traffic coming and going.

After getting back on his block, shit didn't look right and it wasn't jumping at all. Sidney ended up coming thru with about a half ounce of crack but the work wasn't all that but he had to work with it. "This block is dead as fuck, it's like a ghost town over here" Ali tells Lo-Lo

"yeah we got to get the crackheads to come back thru here" Lo-Lo said

"Hell, we would have some traffic coming thru if you wouldn't be beating the customers up when they come thru". Lo-Lo was known for knocking out and beating up crackheads for coming up short or sometimes just for the hell of it.

"I think that I'm going to go on Sprinkle and sell dope for Jet" Lo-Lo states

"Go ahead, but when I get this shit back to jumping don't come back over here and try to jump back on the team."

For the next 2-3 weeks Ali practically stayed on the block in one of the trap houses trying to pump life back into the hood. Shit was just slow and Ali couldn't keep a steady clientele to come thru. He thinks how Homecoming is coming up in a few weeks and he wants to do something big for the event. But the way things were looking his pockets was fucked up. By having to eat every day, put minutes on the phone, get hotel rooms, buying clothes to get his wardrobe back up and paying people to take him places leaves him with just his re-up money, He just thinks that he needs a lick to come up on so he can just get over the hump that he needs to go to the top. And as if it was a sign his nigga DB pulls up. DB -AKA- Demolition Man. He was in the car with Wheat. DB was a nigga that Ali grew up with and use to do jack moves with. They both knew that each other was down for the cause and that they both put in work. "What's up my nigga?" DB says to Ali.

"What up with you my nigga"

"I just seen Wheat at the store and he told me that you were out, why didn't you come holla at me"

"I don't know where you stay at now, you moved out the PJ's"

"I got a case in the car and a gallon of gin, let's get fucked up"

It was nothing else to be said. They sat on the block and got fucked up like old times. Kicking it and talking about what was the going on in the city. "Man, I got to get me something to eat to feed this liquor, let's go to Raymond's and get some fish sandwiches" DB says. When they got to Raymond's and got their fish sandwiches and another case of beer, DB pulls out a fresh $100 bill and Ali says "Damn, it's like that homie" on the way out the store.

"Nah, this my last $100 and I borrowed this from my girl when I heard that you were out, I had to come show my dawg some love and get you fucked up."

"that's what's up my dude" Ali tells him.

When they got back on Dash Street, they continued to drink and kick it about the good old days. After a while it was just Ali, Wheat, and DB left on the block and Ali said, "I got to get some paper, I got to do something"

"I thought that you were never going to ask, I got some heavy licks lined up" DB lets them know. Between the 3 of them they had about 100 serious felonies on their record but none of the charges ever stuck in court because they knew how to get down for theirs. DB goes on to tell them about this kid named Teddy from Santee that was supposed to be moving bricks and getting that paper. The kid was supposed to have race cars, motorcycles and a bunch of cars. DB laid the lick down and told Ali and Wheat about the lay out. When DB finished telling him he asked Ali what was up.

"My Nigga, you know that I'm all in". They looked at Wheat and he said, "When can we do this because I'm ready to eat now". DB lets them know that they can do it that weekend. Ali lets the crew know that he still had all the jack gear from before. He keeps it for times like these. His jack gear consists of everything black. Mask, guns, duct tape, fatigues and duffle bag. They set everything up for the weekend.

Santee, SC

That Saturday night they were waiting behind a shed in the kid Teddy's house for about 3 hours. It was about 2:30 in the morning and DB said, "I'm going to slap the shit out this nigga for having us out here this long" Ali and Wheat laughs but know that he is dead serious. That's how DB got his name Demolition Man, when he gets wound up or excited he turns into a beast and start wrecking shit. If niggas didn't want to give up the goods he will beat them into submission and compliance. They sat in the dark for about 30 more minutes then they saw some car lights coming down the dirt road towards the double wide trailer. "Alright, we going to run down on him when he gets out the car to go in the house" Ali tells them. When the car pulled up to the back yard they could see that in the car was two people, a male and female. "That's Teddy Honda and that's him driving" DB says. "Fuck it we got to get them both" Ali said. But before they could make a move they see the female jump out and head to the house while from the overhead light in the car they can see that Teddy is on the phone. "Shit, we got to wait until that nigga get off the phone." DB says. They all sit back and watch Teddy get off the phone and get out the car but instead of going to the back door, he heads towards the carport that the crew is lying in wait for him. "Fuck it, we going to make him run it in here." Ali says. When Teddy entered the carport all three of the crew jumped out with guns drawn and ran down on Teddy. Teddy threw his hands up in the air and began to beg and plead. He let them know that he had everything in a shoe box on a shelf of the garage. Wheat went over and got the box and brought it back to show DB and Ali. It looked to be about a Big 8 of coke (4 ½ ounces). DB snatched Teddy by the collar and lets him know to stop playing with him and come up off the dope before he won't see another day to sell shit. "that's all I got here" Teddy says in a creaky voice. "we know that you got some money in the house or somewhere nigga" Wheat tells Teddy.

"It's only me and my momma in the house but it's no money."

"Fuck it, I'm about to take this nigga inside and slap this bitch up, I bet she knows where something is at." DB states. After saying that, Teddy must have known that DB was dead serious because he struck out running and screaming for help and for someone to call the police. DB went to pull the trigger to stop the nigga but the safety was on saving Teddy's life. "Fuck it we done fucked up now, we got to go" Ali says as motions for DB to put the gun down, then they took off running in the opposite direction to where they had the car parked waiting on the dirt road.

When they made it back to the Burg they found out they had about 5 ounces of coke. So, they split what they had and went their separate ways for the night. Ali got Rashawn to pick him up to get a room at Ho Jo's (Howard Johnson), while DB and Wheat went to ball out with the coke they had. They snorted cocaine like it was going out of style but Ali didn't get down like that. He stopped smoking dirty's so he could get his money up.

Ali and Rashawn got back to the room after dropping the jack gear off, he sat down and thought about how he risks 20 to 30 years of his life for one punk ass ounce of coke. He said right then that he was just going to try to tough it out and get the money off the grind, he could not jeopardize himself like that and put himself in *danger no more.*

The next day on the block Ali was trying to get the work off. Shit was slow but it was picking up. For the next few days he was moving the lil shit that he got off the lick and what he had before. Ali was thinking where the hell was Wheat because he hadn't seen him in a few days, it wasn't like Wheat because usually he would be thru the block at least once a day. About 4 days later Wheat came on the block.

"What's up my nigga" Ali ask

"It's nothing fool" Wheat responded

"Where the fuck you been at"

"Man, I had this bad bitch from Greenville that I was tricking with, that bitch fuck and suck me so good I couldn't leave for about a week" Wheat said laughing. All Ali could do was shake his head. He knew that Wheat had fucked up the goods that he got off the lick but that was his comrade and he fucks with him to the end. Shit was going kind of smooth. Ali was trying his hardest to breathe life back in the block, but it's hard to resuscitate when the block has been dead for so long.

It was now about 2 weeks away from South Carolina State University Homecoming. That's when the city comes out and everybody try to get their stunt on. With Orangeburg having two historical black universities, niggas from all over come to school or just come to catch one of the bad bitches that goes to school, and with the females that's going to school have come from all over the U.S. to come to one of the universities that they have heard so much about and you know how the game goes. They are away from home and not under their parent's supervision so now they are getting their party on!! Drinking, clubbing and drugging and you know what that leads too. Fucking and sucking. The locals know that so they be out trying to catch and the hoes be throwing. To the chicks, it's like a whole new world because the niggas from the hood be riding and stunting just like the niggas that they see on the videos on 106 and Park and Rap City. So, to the bitches on campus, the niggas from the hood are like stars.

Ali sits back and think what he going to do for homecoming. He wasn't working with nothing but 2 ounces, and he didn't have the money to buy a whip, paint it and throw some shoes on it. Cause that's just how the niggas was going to do it this year just like any other year. 'I can't do this shit, I got to get my weight up' Ali said to himself. His cell phone goes off and he see the caller id says that its DB calling him. "What it do fool" Ali answers and says.

"Where you at" DB asks him.

"Posted up on the block like the light pole, you know how I do"

"Don't go know where, I'm going to get my girl to drop me off over there"

"This ain't no 7 to 11, I'm on da grind 24/7 my nigga, I'm outchea all day everyday"

Ali goes back to thinking what the hell DB got going on and what's on his mind. But knowing Deon Books he knew it was something up. He sat back and caught a few more plays (drug sales) before DB pulls up. "What they do" Ali greets DB when he gets out of the car. DB heads to the cooler and Ali catches another play before he joins him on the porch. "So, what's up" Ali asks DB.

"Shit trying to come up"

"What, you trying to spend some money with your boy?"

"I'm fucked up again, I had to pay my girl car payment so I'm hurting right now,"

"Wheat told me he had a lick for the team, and he supposed to be coming thru in a little bit" Ali told DB. Ali gave DB a gram of coke and told him to roll up a few dirtys. Ali started back smoking with the boys again. They were smoking and drinking and kicking it when Wheat walked thru the path from the back street. "Brace yourself fool" He screams from behind Ali and DB imitating the dude on Menace 2 Society. Ali automatically went for the chrome 357 smith and Wesson. "Wheat you going to fuck right around and get your ass blown back on State Court doing shit like that" they all start to laugh but they do know not to trust Ali's right hand. And it's not because Ali knows how to fight good, it's because he has that trigger finger on that hand and it has a lot of action and practice. Every nigga off Dash Street will tell you that and maybe some unfortunate niggas from across town will tell you. Hell, Ali don't even trust his own right hand because when he blanks out, he loses control and no telling what he will do. If its fighting in the club, that's what it is but when he gets to the parking lot its pistol play. At one time, they were calling him Bishop off juice because back in the days he shot one of his homies after a brief heated argument. "What's up with that thing you were telling me about" Ali asks Wheat. Wheat went on to explain that he wanted to hit the nigga CD off C Block (Coleman Ave). It was all about the niggas CD selling Wheat small sacks of bullshit coke. The way he explained the lick, CD should be working with a block with all the sacks he was selling. "Sounds like a winner" DB smiles ready for action.

"How we going to hit this nigga?" Ali wanted to know.

"We run up in his mama house on C-Block, that's where he sells all them sacks at"

"What about them niggas Whoodie and Ice off C-Block, them niggas be posted up on the block all day everyday" Ali asks Wheat

"Shit, we lay they ass down too if they come down there" Wheat said with a straight face. Ali and DB knew that he was dead serious. John Sharks -AKA- Wheat was about 110 pounds soaking wet but got the heart of a 500-pound gorilla. And that nigga doesn't give a fuck about putting that pistol on a nigga ass. Ali sits back and think about homecoming is coming up and he needs to get right. "Wheat we got to get that nigga some other kind of way then running up in his momma house on C-Block" Ali lets him know.

"Well he fucks with this bitch that stay on Solomon Terrace, he be laid up over there at night"

"He posted up on our turf? Oh, that fuck nigga got to get it." DB said

They set the lick up for the next night. CD was going to get taught a lesson for coming into the lion's den on some other niggas turf. They chop it up for a few and think that the team should be straight if he holding like he should be holding. Then Hassan pulls up and gets out with his old ass New York accent. That nigga done been in Orangeburg about 18 years and he is about 20 years old but he still thinks he from New York. "What's up son" Hassan spits when he gets close. He daps everybody up and grab a bud light out of the cooler. Hassan pulls out a half ounce of coke and begins to roll dirtys. "Let me see that coke, where you get this shit from" Ali asks as he examines it.

"That nigga Polo from Miami, he got clean and he be giving it up" he lets Ali know.

"Oh yeah, where that nigga be at" DB asks

"He took me out to his house in Cordova, but he be doing shit off his landscaping truck or this fruit stand that he has"

"So, what's up" everybody asks in unison

"Anybody can get it" Hassan lets the team know. Hassan didn't grow up on Dash Street, but he fucks with the Dash Street niggas hard. He used to get money with them at the spot-on Aaron street when Jet let him work for him. "I'm telling you that nigga got anything you want"

"Yeah, it's like that"

"Like that"

"So, when can we hit this nigga"

"We can hit that nigga tonight if yall want". Ali, Wheat and DB looks at each other and said I'm all in. Ali got the numbers on what Polo was asking for. Polo was letting the work go for $850 a zone. Ali asked Hassan would he let him get 2 for $1600 and he said that he could do that. "set it up and I'm going to ride with you and see how this nigga look." Hassan hooks it up and they ended up meeting Polo at a spot on the other end of C-Block, Sure enough he is serving off the back of a lawn service truck. When Hassan got back in the car he let them know that Polo said, "Whatever we need, he got it"

"Well we want it all and we going to get it" Wheat screams from the back seat.

"We should get out and nap this nigga now" DB states.

"He does think its sweet out here" Ali says

"Naw, we can't do it like that, its broad daylight and he will see our faces" Hassan said.

"Yeah, we can't stand a 211 right now, they giving out $100,000 bonds for that shit." Ali says

"Let's get that nigga tonight, he will come out if I call him"

"That's what it is then".

They drove back to Dash Street with all of them thinking of what they going to do with the money from the lick they were about to pull. When they got back to the block, Ali broke down one of the ounces and bagged it up while Wheat rolled up a box of philly blunts, all of them heavy laced. That was one of Mike Thomas favorite sayings, "I don't smoke laced, I smoke heavy laced"!!!

They smoked and drank until about dark fall and Ali called Joe from Dash Street crew to give him a ride to get the jack gear.

At the same time, Rashawn was going to get the room for her and her Boo. She already went to the liquor store and got a bottle of Grey Goose for Ali because that was his drink of choice. She already had a black teddy from Victoria Secret that she wants to put on to make her Boo go crazy that night. She put the goose on ice and set everything else up and called Ali and let him know that she was at Howard Johnson in their favorite room. Almost every night they got a room and went crazy fucking each other to sleep. It was a much-needed night cap of hustling on the block every day.

"What's up Boo"

"Nothing, got the room and ready for you". Ali thought that he couldn't go on the lick first and then to Rashawn because she would be waiting all night. So, he decided to go to the room now and fuck Rashawn good and then go on the lick. "Alright, I will be there in a minute." With that, he got Joe to drop him off to the room. Mistake?

When he got to the room and seen how sexy Rashawn looked all he could think about was putting some dick in her and that it was going to take longer than he expected. He dropped the duffle bag on the floor and jumped on the bed with Rashawn. He tried kissing her but she would not let him and kept pushing him away. "What the fuck wrong with you" Ali asked her.

"You up to know good that's whats wrong" she let him know

"What you mean?"

"You know what I mean, you got that bag with all those guns and you about to go kick somebody door and rob them." Ali thought about it and knew that she wasn't stupid and knew what was up.

"Shit, I got to get this money, and if I have to lay a nigga down to get it, that's what it is."

"But you got money"

"4 or 5 grand not real money"

"That's enough money for us, I can deal with the hustling but the robbing is a whole nother level and I got a bad feeling about tonight"

"There you go with that putting bad mouth on a nigga"

"I'm not putting bad mouth on you, and I'm not letting you go nowhere tonight". They argued for about another 20 minutes and Rashawn started crying and begging Ali not to leave her that night. In the end, Ali decided that he would stay with her that night and was thinking what he would tell the team and try to get them to postpone the lick for another night, fuck it here goes nothing Ali thought to himself as he called on the block. DB answers the phone "What's up my nigga"

"It's a change in plans for tonight" Ali said

"What the fuck you mean"

"Rashawn tripping and won't let a nigga leave tonight"

"That shit got to go down tonight, we done made the call and everything is set and ready"

"I can't go tonight"

"That's you, we're going with or without you, lets us get the jack gear"

"come get it"

DB let him know that they would be there in about an hour. Ali went to pour himself a glass of grey goose and cranberry juice and turned to Rashawn and said "you think your ass slick and run shit huh? Well I got something for that ass tonight" and he slapped her on that soft ass real hard and told her to turn the lights off. Ali went to work and being aggressive must have turned Rashawn on because there was no foreplay and she was soaking wet when he stuck his dick inside of her. He was pounding in and out of her with long deep strokes and even thou it was rough and a little painful, Rashawn was loving it. She was trying to throw it back but couldn't so she just held on for the ride. She came about two times before Ali exploded inside of her. They laid there in the bed together and held each other and she let him know that she liked what he just did. They talked for a while before DB and Wheat knocked on the door.

Ali let them in and Wheat said, "Look at this nigga all pussy whipped and can't go nowhere". They all laughed and dapped each other up. "where the gear at because we about to go touch this nigga". Ali gave them the bag and as they were leaving Rashawn told them "Yall be careful now".

"We always careful" Wheat said before they left.

Wheat, DB and Hassan drove to Cordova where the nigga Polo lived with his wife. On the way, they came up with a plan on what they was going to do. Hassan called Polo and let him know that he was on Coleman waiting on him and Polo told him that he would be there in about 5 minutes. "See that's why he got to get it because he knows it's going to take him every bit of 20 minutes to get to C-Block". DB and Wheat got out of the car and went beside the house and waited for Polo to come out. When the front door opened, they crept up and caught him as he was coming down the steps. Wheat slammed the chamber back on the 40 cal and said, "Nigga don't move, and if you do you thru". Polo was like 'damn I got caught slipping and he didn't have a strap on him. "What yall want"

"Nigga you know what it is" DB said as he stepped closer and grabbed him by the collar of his shirt and put the all black Smith and Wesson to his head.

"I don't got shit but a quarter brick on me and a few dollars, that's all I got".

DB slapped him upside the back of his head with the tool and said, "nigga don't play with me, we know you got it, we know everything about you". Wheat put the 40 in his face and asked who was in the house. Polo let them know it was only his wife in the house. "let's take this nigga inside" DB said as he drugged Polo inside and when his wife seen what it was and what was going on she started to scream until DB snatched her ass off the couch. "Bitch don't make me kill your ass in here". That calmed her down real quick. "Let's tie these mutha fuckers up before they get any bright ideas" DB told Wheat and they proceeded to duct tape they asses up. When they finished tying them up they started on asking where the dope and money was at. Polo kept saying that everything was somewhere else and all he had on him was the 9 piece and the only reason he had that was because his wife called him home to eat dinner.

"Well I guess we going to have to take us a little ride and go get this shit" Wheat let him know. DB called Hassan and told him to drive in the yard and pick them up. When he pulled up they put a pillow case over Polo's head and put him in the car. They were wondering what they were going to do with the bitch and they decided to leave her but pulled out the phone wires because they figured she couldn't go anywhere.

After they got in the car and was driving down 301 they started asking Polo where was the dope and money. Polo must have gotten balls from somewhere because he kept saying "Yall might as well kill me now because yall not getting shit, yall going to kill me anyway". So that sent DB over the edge and he started beating him in the backseat and when he got tired Wheat would beat him and they took turns all the way down 301, from Cordova to Orangeburg. When they got in the Burg Wheat told Hassan to drive to Laquinta Drive where it was quiet and they could get the nigga to talk. They pulled on the right side of the road by a cotton field and took Polo out the car and dragged him into the field and started questioning him again. He was still refusing to give up anything. So, Wheat shot him in one of the legs and he let out a scream but still would not give up any info on the whereabouts of the dope or money. Wheat let DB know that he was going to get Hasson to take him back to the house to get the bitch and see if that would make him talk or come up with something. As soon as he got out of the field he heard a loud 'BOOM'. He looked back and then ran to where he left DB and Polo at and ask DB what happened and DB said, "I think I missed and shot him in the head" So Wheat pulled out his phone to get some light so that he could see and sure enough Polo was dead as a doorknob with a hole in his head.

"What the fuck happened" Wheat asked

"I was trying to slap him upside the head and make the gun go off at the same time but I think I missed".

"That nigga got a hole in his head, you didn't miss shit".

"I mean I miss the ground, I wasn't trying to kill him"

"Fuck it, let's go get the bitch and see if we can get her to tell us where something is at". When they got back to Cordova and pulled on the road where the house was located they saw that the wife had gotten loose and was in the yard with the police. It was another fucked up mission.

The next morning Ali got Rashawn to drop him off on Dash Street and when he got to the trap the only person there was Wheat. "What's going my nigg" Ali asked.

"Over here trying to get some paper"

"So yall didn't go on the lick last night"

"Yeah, but everything went sour on us". Wheat went on to explain what went down the night before. Ali asked what they did with the straps and he told him that they dumped them in Edisto River. Before Ali could say anything, Wheat let him know that the rest of the gear was in the backroom and that they were going to pay to replace the straps that got lost on the mission last night. Wheat let him know that he was going to go to his sister house on C-Block and he would hit him up later.

CHAPTER 3
M.O.E. — MONEY OVER EVERYTHING

While on the block Ali sat by himself and started to think how the scene played out last night. He could see that Miami nigga telling DB he wasn't giving up shit and DB putting one in his head. He sat and thought about all the humps that him, DB and Wheat put in the ground and couldn't do nothing but laugh and say fuck it, it's part of the game. He decided to hit DB up and see what he was up too. DB answered on the 2nd ring "What they do" DB yelled.

"Trying to do me" Ali hit back. "You coming thru the block today?"

"I done been up all night getting skeed up, I can't move".

"Alright, I'm going to come thru and holla at you later".

"Alright, I will be here".

Ali caught a few more plays before he called Rashawn to pick him up and drop him off at DB's house.

"What's going on my nigga"

"Trying to keep my face out the sun and the newspaper" DB went to the kitchen and grabbed a few Bud lights out of the refrigerator and came back and turned the tv and PlayStation on so they could play some Madden.

"Nigga I know you about to lay low for a while" Ali asked

"I don't go nowhere so this is as low as I'm going to get, but we still going to hit that nigga CB tomorrow night thou". Ali just looked at him like he was crazy.

"Damn, I thought yall came up last night"?

"We didn't really get shit, and besides we done put the plan together"

"Fuck it, it is what it is" Ali and DB kicked it for a while and played the game before Ali called Rashawn to come pick him up.

When Ali got back on the block Wheat, Hassan and Lil C was there. They were sitting around smoking and drinking and catching sales. Then a crack-head came thru and was like they found a body on Laquninta drive. Wheat, Hassan and Ali gave each other a look of you know what it is but Lil C was none the wiser. That was a rule that they had, if you didn't go on a mission or had anything to do with it, you didn't need to know about it. They all started to talk about hitting the lick on the nigga CD off C-Block. They all decided to go on C-Block to Wheat sister house to see the spot and to see what the nigga CD was working with.

When they got over there, they all saw the traffic going and coming on that block. They were going to Ice and Whoodie spot as well as CD mother's house. "I told you that nigga CD was getting it" Wheat said. They all chilled for a minute before Wheat asked Ali was he strapped and Ali responded, "And you know it" and pulled out the all black snub nose 357 with the black rubber grip. "Why what's up"

"I'm about to go down there and lay Whoodie and Ice down"

"Wheat you wild as hell, them niggas cool"

"I know, I'm just going to scare the shit out they ass thou".

Ali passed the gun to Wheat and he went down the block. Ali, Hassan and Lil C watched as Wheat engaged in a conversation with the niggas off C-Block and then pulled out the 357. From where they were at it looked like Wheat was pulling a jack move on Ice and Whoodie in broad daylight, but then they saw him start to laugh and put the gun away. Wheat stayed down the block for a few more minutes and then walked back up the block. He started laughing and said, "I had them niggas shook" Ali shook his head thinking that nigga is unstoppable.

It was late when they all got back on Dash St. DB came over about 11:30 and they all sat around and smoked and drank. Everybody in their own thoughts. DB was thinking about moving him and his baby moms to another spot. Hassan was thinking about the next bitch he was going to fuck. Lil C was thinking about where he was going to get his next bag of coke from. Wheat was thinking about the next lick and about how straight he was going to be and Ali was thinking about getting that paper... BIG PAPER!!

Getting CD....

That next night all the niggas were on Dash St getting into jack mode. Little did Ali know was that Lil C, which was Rashawn's cousin had let it slip that they were about to do a lick. Lil C was trying to get $20 out of Rashawn to get him a dub sack of coke and told her that he was going to pay her back as soon as him and Ali them hit the lick. So, while everybody was getting shit together and planning on how to do the robbery, Rashawn pulled up and called Ali outside. She tells him to jump in the car and ride somewhere with her. So, when they pulled off he peeped that CD was at the bitch house on Solomon Terrance in his white Cadillac. A big smile goes across his face and all he could see was dollar signs. While riding up 601 she lets him know what the deal was and she was not letting him do that shit that night either. She told Ali that she would follow him all night if she had too. "Yeah nigga, Lil C said he was going to do a kick door and I see his ass right over there on Dash St. so I know what time it is" Ali tries to throw her off but she wasn't going for it. She insists on getting a room and chilling for the night. He thought about it and said she was right but told her to take him back on the block so that he could leave his pistol over there. When they got back on the block, Wheat, Hassan, DB and Lil C was ready for war. He let them know that he wasn't riding again that night but let them know that he saw the nigga CD posted up where they thought he was going to be and it looked extra sweet. Wheat screamed out "Fuck it, it's not going down now but right now"!! Then he asked Ali for the 357 because he wasn't going to need it, and Ali gave it to him with no problem. Mistake

Hassan, Lil C and Wheat jumps in Hassan's sister Honda and heads over to where CD is laid up at. DB and Wheat jumps out the car in Roosevelt Gardens and took the path that connected the PJ's and the Gardens while Hassan and Lil C circled the block.

BOOM! The front door of the mobile home flew open. DB and Wheat charges in the house and heads to the main room to the left of the front door where they saw the light from the outside. Once in the room and they saw CD and the bitch on bed looking scared as hell. "Don't turn this into a murder scene, we just want the money and dope" DB lets them know. CD was acting like he couldn't talk but the bitch couldn't keep her mouth closed. "Craig, give them what they want, yall please don't hurt me, I got kids" she kept saying.

She was telling the robbers that she told CD not to bring drugs into her house and all kinds of shit they didn't want to hear. CD was still stuck on stupid and not saying a word and acting like he couldn't hear. So, DB walked over and snatched a butt naked CD out the bed and put the 40 cal in his face. Suddenly CD could talk and said that the money was in his pants pocket on the floor. Wheat grabs the pants off the floor and pulls a very small not out. "What the fuck is this"

"that's all I got"

"Nigga I know you holding and I am not about to play with you"

"That's all I got"

"Fuck it, let's see what this bitch got to say" Wheat yells

"Jackie" the chick says

"Why the fuck you in the bed with all your jewelry on" DB asks. She is shaking her head because she knows what is about to happen.

"Take that shit off" DB heads towards her but then thinks about it. He didn't come there for no cheap ass jewelry.

"We want the money and dope" DB points the 40 back at CD who is now kneeling in front of the bed.

"I told yall, I don't have nothing man" CD pleads.

"We not leaving until we get it nigga" DB responds. Wheat gets tired of the back and forth and tells DB to kill him just like he killed Miami Polo. That was like music to DB ears because he gets a big smile and raises the gun to CD's head and then CD finally told them that the drugs were at his mother's house in a shoe box in the closet. "Well we about to go pay your mother a little visit" DB lets him know. He tells Wheat to tie the bitch up good this time. "Matter fact, call ol' boy out the car to sit in here with her until we come back". Wheat goes outside and calls Hassan and tell him what the plan is and tell him to hurry up and come thru. When Hassan pulls up and jumps out the Honda, Wheat and DB put CD in his own Cadillac takes him to his momma's house. On the way there, CD begs them not to hurt his momma and that she will not come out the back room. He lets DB know which key was the key to open the door and which way to go in once inside. They pull up to the house and parked in the front yard. DB jumps out while Wheat holds CD at gun point. Two things went wrong. First, they pulled up to a drug spot in CD's car and second when the cluckers and tweekers saw that, they came over to cop or beg for something. While DB was trying to get the door open, fiends kept asking was he straight thinking he was CD. When they notice that he was too big to be CD they went over to the car and began to tap on the window calling out CD's name. Wheat gets irritated and lets the window down and puts the gun out the window and tell the fiends to get the fuck away from the car. With all the commotion going on DB could not concentrate and decides to abort the mission. He jumps off the porch and gets back into the car and pulls off fast as hell. "We should take this nigga ass and dump him on Laquinta Drive stinking" Wheat says.

"Naw, we got to go back and get Hassan out the house".

They pull back up and DB picks CD up by himself and carries him into the house. They tell Hassan to come on and they dip back to the projects. Once they get back to Roosevelt Gardens, Wheat realize that he does not have his gun. "Hold up, you got my gun" Wheat asks DB

"Naw, you don't got it?"

"Damn, I think I left it in the car". They decide to go back and get it but when they came out of the pathway, CD was in his Caddy headed back up 601 towards C-Block. "DAMN" is all that Wheat could say.

When they all met back up on Dash Street the next day and talked about how the lick went down, Ali got pissed and a little stressed out about the fact they left the 357 at the scene of the crime. "How the fuck did yall do that" Ali asks.

"I don't know, we were trying to get the nigga back in the house, but fuck that nigga, what he going to tell the cops we robbed him for some dope" Wheat says in a nonchalant way. Ali went on a rant about she called the police and he wasn't sure if his finger prints were on the gun or not. In the end, everybody was like fuck it, if they come they come.

Homecoming 2002:

"What they do" Ali ask Joe from the barbershop on Dash Street. "you next" Joe lets him know he was next in the chair. Once he sat down in the chair he lets the barber know that he wanted a low ceaser. "the city is pack, what you getting into today" Joe asks Ali while he is getting his haircut right.

"I got a rental, room and some money in my pocket so it's no telling what I will get into today"

"Be careful out there because the police are really bad out there"

"Good looking, I got you". After getting lined up proper Ali goes back up to the trap where everybody is at. Ali, Wheat, Hassan and Chin all decide to ride thru the campus to see what its hitting for with the bitches on State and Claflin. "Damn son, shit is jumping for real out here" Hassan says with his New York accent. All of them are just looking at the fine ass hoes that's walking around until Ali sees a burgundy ford escort is flashing its light at them. "Who the fuck is that" he says out loud as he grabs the bulldog (snub nose 44) from under the seat.

"I think that C-Lo ole lady Sonya" Chin lets them know. "pull over to the Bojangles store". Sonya gets out and approaches the car and let them know the word on the streets.

"You know they say that yall the ones that kidnap CD, the other night right"

"Who the fuck said something like that"

"Jamie, Whoodie baby mama said he told her that the Dash St. boys did it and they know for sure that it was Wheat because the same gun he was show-ing them the day before is the one CD found in the car after the robbery". Ali looks at Wheat like I told you so nigga.

"Them niggas tripping, we didn't do that shit" Wheat tells Sonya.

"Well Whoodie and Ice say yall did it and they wish that yall would try some shit like that with them because they stay strap" Sonya lets the Dash St. boys know. Wheat gets excited and starts bouncing up and down in the seat and tells Ali "Lets ride thru C-Block and shoot that shit up since they strap with all that mouth".

"Don't do that because Jamie be over there with them kids" Sonya pleads with them, more so to Wheat because he is the one that is amped up.

"We not fucking with them niggas, we didn't do that shit so fuck em, if they want to come see us, they know where to find us all day everyday" Ali lets her know.

"Alright, I will holla at yall later, I just wanted to let yall know what's up. Yall do know that I got an apartment over by the Armory and yall can come chill if yall want to". They all let her know that they may come over and break the spot in.

"I knew that I should have robbed them niggas when I had the chance" Wheat says out loud.

"Them niggas cool but they can get it" Chin says

"I know they got money, real money" Ali chimes in

"let's hit them niggas then" Hassan speaks up

"Naw, fuck them niggas, let them live" Ali asks

"Ok, but if them niggas come out their mouth sideways again, I'm laying that ass down." Wheat puts it out there.

That night DSP went to Shorty's Club to party. "Damn, I don't like going down this long ass dirt road and getting my car dirty and shit" Ali says

"Shut the fuck up, this a rental and you wash this shit like it's your car" Wheat says with a loud laugh and everybody burst out laughing because they know the statement is true. "I'm about to roll a whole box of dirty's to take in the club. Wheat says. By the time they reached the parking lot he had all the dirty's rolled. Ali peeps the parking lot and sees all the Chevy's and caddy's on rims and says, "next year I'm going to be riding big". In the club, in between cups of Grey Goose and Budlights a thick chic named Cupcake off the fairground rolls up on Ali and tells him

"You know your bitch been fucking my baby daddy while you were locked up"

"Who my bitch"

"Rashawn over there by the bar" she says as she points directly at Rashawn at the bar ordering a drink.

"So, who is your baby daddy?"

"Aaron, off Sprinkle". Ali shakes his head and then thinks back at the times he has seen Aaron since he got out and thinks he sees a smirk on his face every time. Before Cupcake walks off she lets him know he needs to stop fucking with them lil girls and fuck with a real woman while strutting away swinging that fat ass.

Ali sat there uptight and mad as hell thinking about the cross he just heard about. He orders another pitcher of goose and cranberry and started drinking heavy. Rashawn came over a little tipsy and ask him is she going home with him tonight. "FUCK NO, you better go home with that nigga Aaron that you been fucking" Ali said with venom in his voice. And the look and no response that she gave him let him know that it was true. She asked him to go outside so they could talk.

"It's not shit to talk about, get the fuck out my face before I catch a CDV". She sees the anger in his face and just walked off.

After the club, they all headed to the Waffle House on 601. On the way, up there they spotted Aaron in is sprite colored dunk with spinners on it with some of his do boys in his other Chevy behind him. "I'm going to kidnap that nigga Aaron when we get to the waffle house" He says. Everybody else in the car just laugh it off not taking it serious, until Chin looks over and see Ali with that bulldog in his lap gripping it tightly and his jaw muscles moving. "Ali, I know what it is but you can't do it like that, it's too many people out there and you don't have a mask on"

"Fuck it, that nigga ain't going to make it back to tell nobody shit"

"Naw Ali, I know what this is really about because my girl told me already but I know how you get that's why I didn't tell you cause of how you acting now". Chin says, he went on to say "Look my nigga, if the bitch didn't get rape that means she gave the pussy up, so why be mad at the nigga?". Ali thinks about it for a minute while riding in silence. "You know what you right, I'm all about getting some BIG PAPER, FUCK EVERYTHING ELSE"

MONEY OVER BITCHES!!! MONEY OVER EVERYTHING!!!!!

CHAPTER 4
DA COME UP

November 2002

"What's up Sonya" Ali says.

"You know that C-lo been calling trying to catch up with you"

"Let him know I'm chasing that money, I ain't got time to sleep or talk".

She went on to explain that when she went to see him over the weekend he was talking about Ali and was like they never be on the streets at the same time together for long and how they are the closest of the rest of them, and he didn't want Ali to fuck around and get locked up on them bogus as licks. "let that nigga know that I'm straight and will be here when he touchdown." Ali let her know

Shit got hot over on Dash St., with the jump out boys coming thru and jumping out almost every day when they got a wift that it was back booming. So, the DSP crew took Sonya up on her offer and started chilling at her apartment. It didn't take long for that spot to get jumping. Jet, C-lo's brother had traffic coming thru, Aaron off Sprinkle had traffic coming thru and the DSP crew was just wilding out.

"You need to stop selling that blow-up dope and buy some of this straight drop that I got" Jet tells Ali while showing him a cookie (28 grams of crack).

"Shit, as long as it sells I don't give a fuck because I don't smoke the shit" Ali tells Jet and laugh while leaving out the apartment.

"What you laughing at" Hassan asks as Ali jumps in Sonya car. Sonya is a real ride or die chick, she lets the crew drive her car to make plays.

"That nigga Jet trying to get a nigga to buy that high as dope he got, I guess he see how a nigga moving that work." Ali says

"All them niggas on Sprinkle are haters and that's my brother and he still drag the shit out of me, I'm going to rob his ass he keeps playing" Chin says laughing but serious at the same time.

"That nigga still owe me for all that dope I use to sell for him, I want to rob that ass too." Hassan says with grimy ass.

"He still owes you too?' Chin says and then said, 'that's why when his ass be sleep I be going right in them pockets" let it be known that when Jet be sleeping he clips his pockets for about $200-$300 and he don't miss it.

"Hassan, take me to the House Of Pizza so I can meet Greek, he wants a half" Ali yells from the back seat.

They pull up to the House of Pizza on John C. Calhoun by the Hot Spot. After getting a table and ordering their food the crew just sat back and chilled and talked about what they were going to do that night.

"It's Wednesday and I don't got shit going on" Wheat says.

"I know I'm just going to hug the block tonight and make money" Ali says

"That's all you want to do is ride around and sell dope all day and all night" Chin speaks

"Ain't shit else to do"

"I'm going to my baby mamas house in the gardens, you know I got to plea to that baby life sentence (YOA) next role call" Chin lets them know. After leaving the House of Pizza they drive over to the gardens and Ali and Chin gets out the car to go into the apartment.

"I'm about to beat this bitch ass when we get in there" Chin tells Ali

"For what"

"This bitch be taking all my money and losing it at the card games". Ali could do nothing but shake his head because he knew Chin and he knew that he would beat a bitch and caught CDV's all the time. So, he decided to call his cousin Javon to come pick him up, and he was already in the projects so that was perfect because Ali did not feel like playing referee because even thou Chin baby mama Tisha was a female, she could throw down like a man.

Ali and Javon just drove around and got fucked up smoking and drinking. "Javon, take me over on Sprinkle to see if I see Ra-Ra". On the way over, Javon shows Ali a tech 22 that he had. He likes it and remembers putting in some work with one. One night after C-lo brother got killed some niggas was talking slick at the club on Dash St. territory 'The Ritz'. "I lit a nigga ass up with one of these, they don't have no knock down power but they spit pretty good". They pulled up to this smoker named Rena house on Sprinkle where all the Sprinkle boys was hustling at. Ali winds the window down and tells Ra-Ra to come over to the car. Ra-Ra, Lo-Lo and Escobar was on the porch snorting cocaine. "Ali that's you? You still got some of that good good you had the other night?"

"come on nigga, you know I got you"

"Damn, you don't fuck with your boy no more" Lo-Lo screams from the porch. Ali looks at Lo-Lo and see that he is higher than a Georgia pine and says, "What the fuck you talking about"

"You always come thru and pick Ra-Ra up but you don't fuck with me"

"Nigga you crazy as hell, I thought you couldn't leave off the block"

"Take a nigga to the store". Even though he didn't want too he told Lo-Lo to come on. When he did that, Lo-Lo just invited Escobar to come with them.

As soon as they pull off, the bullshit started. "Damn, you don't fuck with your dawg no more" Lo-Lo says again. Ali starts to think where is all the bull-shit is coming from. What he didn't know was that when Jet comes on the block he lets Lo-Lo and them know that he was getting money and that they should be more like him instead of fucking up packs (drug packages that gets fronted) And it's no better when Ra-Ra gets picked up and come back and let them know how good the coke is that Ali has.

"Since you got home from jail you been on some other shit" Lo-Lo goes in again.

"I am on some other shit, I'm trying to get money, I am not with that bull-shit". Ali lets Lo-Lo know.

"That's supposed to be your dawg, yall supposed to get money together" Escobar butts in.

"What they fuck you mean, he doesn't chill with me, he be over here doing what he does"

"Let a nigga get something" Lo-Lo asks

"Let you get something? For what, so you can fuck it up?" Ali says not liking the way the conversation is going. He hopes they hurry up and make it to the store so he can drop Escobar and Lo-Lo back off. Drugs and alcohol impairs the brain and how one thinks. One may do something that they don't normally do.

"I told yall he doesn't fuck with a nigga no more" Lo-Lo says as he pushes Ali in the back of the head.

"What the fuck wrong with you nigga, who the fuck you think I am". Ali turns around in the front seat to look in the back.

"You don't fuck with me, you ain't my dawg" Lo-Lo says.

Ali is pissed by this time and says, "Fuck it then, you better find something to play with because you put your hands on me again, I will light your ass up".

"We got guns too" Escobar says putting gas on the fire while showing Ali bullshit Hi-Point 9mm.

"But I will bust mine though" Ali says pissed and just put it out there. Escobar and Ra-Ra never seen Ali get down but heard about him but Lo-Lo knows all too well how Ali gets down. On numerous occasions Ali had to bust his gun to get niggas off Lo-Lo or to get at niggas over some shit that he started. Now since being around another set of niggas, wanting to impress them and being high as hell kept him going "Nigga you not going to do shit" Lo-Lo says as he mushes Ali in the back of the head again. Ali gets mad and snatches the Tech-22 from under seat, turns around and swung it in the back seat where Lo-Lo, Ra-Ra and Escobar was. All three of them went to ducking and Ra-Ra pushes the barrel up and Escobar yells "don't shoot in the car, you fuck around and hit all of us". At this time, they are going over the railroad track by Whittaker Elementary school so Ali tells his cousin to pull over on the side road right at the tracks. He is beyond pissed and threatens Lo-Lo "Nigga if you get out the car, I'm going to kill your ass". As soon as the car stops Ali jumps out and Lo-Lo being high and wanting to show his Sprinkle boys he is not scared, jumps out the other side of the car. When Lo-Lo stepped around the corner, Ali let it rip on his former Dash St. partner, going back to being Bishop. It sounded like mini firecrackers going off but Lo-Lo was so high that he is still coming forward towards Ali trying to fight until after the 6th or 7th shot then it starts to register to his brain the he is being shot. Ali is so mad at him for trying him like that, that he aims at his face to take a shot but Lo-Lo raises his hand to block it and catches a bullet in his hand. By this time, Escobar and Ra-Ra gets out the car and the shooting has stopped. The sight of Lo-Lo still standing and its dark outside they don't believe that he is shot. Escobar says, "That nigga got a play-play gun".

"Naw, that nigga done shot me for real" says Lo-Lo. Everybody just stood in silence, Ali started to come to his senses and puts the empty tech back in the car. Lo-Lo is too high to feel the real effects of being shot so he goes on another verbal assault and threatens to kill Ali for shooting him, Ali blanks again and asks his cousin does he have any more bullets so he could finish him off, his cousin wisely says no. Then Ali remembers that Escobar has the high point "let me get that gun so I can finish this nigga off". Escobar does not want to give it up so he declines and says "Yall homeboys, yall not supposed to shoot each other."

Ali was not trying to hear that and was ready to get at Lo-Lo. Ra-Ra is trying to calm the situation down and get him to go take Lo-Lo to the hospital. Ali didn't give a fuck at first and just wished the nigga dropped dead, then thinks about it and told his cousin to take him to the hospital.

Ra-Ra and Ali decides to go to Ra-Ra mother's house on Myers road to get her car. They walk thru the path on the other side of the track and got the car. Once in the car Ra-Ra looks at Ali and says, "They told me you was fool up, but bitch you crazy for real, you said you was going to shoot him and you shot the shit out of him." Then started laughing. Ali and Ra-Ra rode around for a couple hours getting drunk and high. They stopped by bootleg lady Goldie house several times to get 5th's of Hennessey. About 4 hours after the shooting Ra-Ra asked Ali where he wanted to be dropped off at because he was going back on Sprinkle. Ali was so fucked up that he said, "Fuck it, I'll ride over there with you".

When they pulled up to Rhonda's house on Sprinkle, Escobar, Gram (Lo-Lo) cousin and a few other Sprinkle niggas was standing in the yard. They all are looking at Ali like I know this nigga is not back on our turf after shooting one of our peoples. Ali was so jacked up that he could give a fuck what they thought or the danger he is in. He jumps out of the car and says, "What's up" and goes on the side of the house to take a piss. While relieving himself, Gram sneaks up behind him smacks him in the back of the head with a gun. What Ali didn't know was that Lo-Lo was in the house trying to come down off his super high, he snatched the iv's out at the hospital and just walked out. Grams goes inside and gets his cousin and lets him know who he has outside knocked out. They both begin to kick, beat and pistol whip an unconscious Ali. Ra-Ra tries to stop the assault by grabbing one, but when he does so, the other goes to work on Ali. After they get tired of beating him, Ra-Ra gets him up but he still has that same attitude and says, "I'm going to kill you niggas".

When he comes to, Ali realizes that he is in the hospital and his bed is surrounded by Sidney, Sonya, Wheat and DB. They all have tears in their eyes and Sidney asks, "Lil Bro, what they fuck happen to you?"

"I don't know, all I remember was I was last on Sprinkle".

"I'm going to kill all them niggas" Wheat says and DB says, "I told you not to trust them niggas". Everybody was ready for war. Nobody knew for sure what happened the night before but they did know that Ali was in the hospital and that didn't sit well with any of them.

"The doctor only gave us a few minutes, so you got to rest up, by the way Rashawn is upfront and wants to see you but didn't know if you wanted to see her"

"Yeah, send her back here". As soon as she walks in, she breaks down in tears at the sight of him. Ali is wondering why when everybody sees him they be in tears, so he gets up to check himself out in the mirror and when he does, he breaks down himself and vows to put the niggas to sleep whenever he sees them.

Rashawn is practically staying in the hospital and at Ali's house once he was released helping him back to good health. They are fucking like rabbits with all the time they are spending together. He is damn near broke now from not hustling and the loss of the sweet 16 (1/16 of a kilo, 62 grams) that he lost the night he went into the hospital. Wheat, DB, and Hassan comes to Ali moms house in the country to holla at him. Ali sends Rashawn in the other room because he knows that they about to talk about some real shit. "I been rolling thru Sprinkle but I don't be seeing Lo-Lo or Gram out there" Wheat says

"They know what time it is" DB states

"My sister Towanna said she seen Lo-Lo in the Pub the other night and he said that I flipped on him for no reason and shot him". Ali said

"Oh yeah, that nigga be at the Pub" DB asks

"Yeah we going to catch him at Sunday Night Explosion and I'm going to let the gun explode on his ass this time" Ali says wickedly as he grabs the SKS from beside the bed.

Ali calls Sonya to pick him up and take him to her apartment where everybody is at. "C-Lo said he don't want everybody over to my apartment like that but you and his brothers" Sonya tells him. On the way to the apt. he is in deep thought about how he almost ended up dead and was all the way off point slipping. So, he decides then to never touch a dirty again. She dropped him off to her apartment and tells him to be careful and that she is going to work at K-Mart. She also lets him know that the niggas off Sprinkle will smile in his face and be talking shit behind his back. He takes it all in and shakes his head in acknowledgement.

As Ali is walking in, Jet is leaving out and says, "What's up Rambo, I see you out of hiding?"

"Yeah I'm back but I am not slipping this time" he says and shows Jet the 357 that he has on him. He felt as if he had to show him just in case if Jet went on Sprinkle and let them niggas know where he was at. Jet must have sensed that also because he said, "Them niggas know not to come over here with that bullshit, I told them I be over here and my brother girl so if they wanted to take it there that they got to catch in you in the streets"

"They going to catch a few hollow points fucking with me". After that he went ahead in the apartment.

Wheat and Hassan looked like they had something on their mind. "What the fuck wrong with yall"

"That niggas Jet be trying to handle a nigga, now he tripping talking about if we not selling dope for him then we can't hang over here" Hassan states clearly pissed off.

"Fuck that, I be damn if I let a nigga pimp me." Wheat says. Then Hassan let it be known about his intentions. "I done hit DB up and let him know I'm going to rob his ass"

"You know fucking with DB and Jet being so stingy he not going to give it up and he can't take no beating from DB" Ali laughs

"Anybody can get it, and he off Sprinkle so fuck em" Hassan says. Ali is amazed at what is about to go down so he asked how he planned to rob him. Hassan let him know that Jet took them out to his trailer in the country and they were going to catch him just like they caught Miami Polo. Ali thought about it and said fuck it because he felt like he didn't have shit to do with it and wasn't going to stop it because Jet tried to fuck Rashawn while he was locked up so all of it was fair game.

Later that night in Swansea, SC

Wheat, Hassan, and DB are in Swansea at Jet trailer ready to pull the caper. "Let's go in from the back and wait for them to come in". Hassan says.

"How you know they not coming thru the back?" Wheat asks.

"Because he says it's too dark back here and he don't use the back door". Hassan says as he breaks the black glass and enters the mobile home. They lay in wait until their victims come home.

Meanwhile in Orangeburg at the 'Pub'

"Damn DJ Cleve got this bitch jumping with Sunday Night Explosion" Ali says to Sidney.

"It's pack as hell out here" he agrees. They are sitting in a stolen box Chevy that they got Nick off the hilltop to steal for this mission. "I'm going to have that nigga Lo-Lo dancing when I hit him with this chopper" Ali grits while gripping the SKS.

"We going to make sure his ass is dead this time, even if we got to back up and get out and let him have it." The plan was as soon as the spot Lo-Lo that Sidney would roll up on him and Ali would hang out the window and let loose and rip Lo-Lo apart. About 20 minutes later they see the club door burst open and a large crowd come bailing out and looked like a big fight was going on.

"Crank up bro, if I'm right and that's a fight, then Lo-Lo is in the middle of it." While scanning the parking lot they see that it looks like niggas off Hwy 4 are beefing with the Sprinkle boys. "There he goes right there, pull up beside him" Ali points out Lo-Lo.

Before they could get to where Lo-Lo was at, they see Ra-Ra pull out a gun and start busting at the Hwy 4 niggas. Cars start racing all over the parking lot, people are screaming and running and Ali sees somebody drop like they got hit and it's one of the Highway 4 niggas. One of dude partners scoop him up and puts him in a car and pull off. "I hear police sirens". "Can you get a good shot?" Sidney asks Ali.

"Naw that nigga to far over, pull off before the cops get here."

Back in Swansea

"Damn you sure somebody stay here, it ain't shit in the refrigerator?" asks Wheat as he goes thru the refrigerator.

"Why don't we wait outside to see if he strap when he gets out the car and then force him back in the house". DB says. A few minutes after they get out the house the spot some car lights coming up the dirt road. As the grey Honda pulls in the yard they realize its Jet girl Shakira by herself. "What yall want to do, snatch the bitch up and wait until Jet gets here?" DB asks as Shakira is getting out the car.

"Naw let's wait until he pulls up and then go in" Wheat says.

"I think we should snatch Kira ass up and strip her and tie her up" Hassan says out loud.

"I bet your freaky ass want to do something like that" Wheats speaks up.

"She does have a fat ass in them jeans and I been wanting to see what she's working with"

"Shhh, I think she's looking over here and she pulled out her cellphone" DB says in a hush toned as they watch her dial a number on her phone and heads in the house. "Creep to the front of the house and see what's going on" DB instructs Hassan. A few minutes later he comes back and says, "She was on the phone with Jet and she thinks something is up and scared to leave out the front room but she did tell Jet to hurry up and come home, he also told her to be in a bra and panties when he gets here but she wasn't trying to hear that".

Wheat cell vibrates in his pockets and looks at the caller ID and see that its Ali. "What up" Wheat says in a low whisper.

"Nigga I was trying to put a nigga lights out and then all hell broke loose at the Pub. I'm trying to catch a body and I think they put a tag on a nigga toe" Ali laughs at his own joke.

"Oh Yeah" Wheat whispers.

"Why the fuck you whispering, you tricking or something? says Ali.

A-Town

"We up at the spot and Jet bitch in the house now". Wheat says. Ali starts to think and realize that his niggas are not playing no games. He gets a bad vibe about it and tell them to leave it alone and come back to the Burg. Wheat agrees that shit wasn't going right that night and went back to where DB and Hassan was at and let them know about the mission. It took a minute but they all decided to leave but before they left Hassan took some duct tape and left in on the back porch to let Jet know he was next! It was the same duct tape that they used on Miami Polo!!!

CHAPTER 5
REAL RECOGNIZE REAL

A few days later...

"Lil Bro, what's up?" Sidney asks Ali.

"Ain't shit, just looking for a better way"

"My cousins down in Eutawville say it's this kid down there getting some real paper"

"What you trying to pull a caper"

"No, he supposed to be some kind of kin to me and they say the prices are lovely, I think his name is Twan C or some shit like that"

"I was locked up with a nigga from down that way when I was at Mac-Dougal before I got shipped" Ali let Sidney know.

"Get your money together, we going to ride down there to see what we can come up with".

They got Sonya to drive them down to Eutawville. On the way, down there Ali was in deep thoughts, he was thinking about all the paper he heard was down there in the country from niggas he was locked up with and thinking how Lo-Lo was locked up for murder. He didn't feel no way about it but he felt Lo-Lo would rather be dead than catch a L for that body. He also was still not comfortable until Gram was put to sleep. Ali looked into the mirror and sees all the scars on his face and thinks about the slow death he will bring to them niggas when he catches up with them.

When they pulled up to the trap spot, they looked at each other dumb-founded. The scene was unreal. Cars was coming back and forth like a Mc-

Donalds drive thru. "I don't know what he is doing but he's doing something" Sidney says out loud. Ali surveys the area, it's a brand new double wide and single wide trailer on the property. At least 30 pit bulls placed all over the property on chains and then there was a small tent where everybody was going too. "You see the nigga" Sidney asks.

"Naw, let's go over by the tent" says Ali. As they get out the car, Twan C spots Ali and yell out "What's up playboy". They embrace tight and Twan C says, "The last time I saw you, you was knocking them Gangsta Disciple niggas out on the yard left and right".

"I told you them niggas couldn't fuck with me, this my brother Sidney right here" Ali says and points his brother out. They dap each other up and Sidney let him know who his peoples was down that way. "What's up, yall niggas good" Twan C asks.

"We trying to get some work, and we heard that you got it for the low down here." Sidney speaks up.

"I got em for 7.5 all day."

"Let me get two of them" Sidney say

"Hardball or softball"

"Split it"

Before he could get what Sidney ordered he had to take care of about 4 more customers that was already in the tent. Ali witness Twan C get down. He is taking coke out of bags and putting them into beakers and throwing them into the microwave without a scale! Damn the boy is good. He finishes up with the others and then gives Sidney what he asked for. Then Twan C turns and give Ali what looks to be a cookie and an ounce of coke. "That's for you my nigga, you don't owe me shit. Just shop with your boy".

"That's what's up Real Recognize Real" says Ali. On the way, back to Orangeburg, Ali feels like it's know excuse now, he has no choice but to come up.

Chapter 6
Murder On My Mind

Over the next few days and weeks, Ali is doing his thing. Moving that dope. Although its 20's and grams and half of slabs at the most but he is going thru the work like crazy. Ali is taking trips to Eutawville at least once a day and sometimes 2 and 3 times. Ali is also breaking bread with Hassan and Wheat. He sells them weight or fronts a little weight for them to bring the money back. Ali is in Sonya's car on the hill making all kind of plays. Ali and Sonya are real close and she lets him get the car whenever he feels like it because she can see that he is on the grind and that he is her nigga right hand man. Ali so much trust Sonya that he gives her his money to put up. Ali pulls up on Treason St where Sonya apartment is located and is headed inside when Wheat and Hassan pulls up. "What they do" Ali asks.

Wheat is super excited. "I just went thru Sprinkle and I saw that fuck boy walking to Mets store".

"You know what it is then, let me take Sonya her keys and give her this food" says, Ali. It wasn't nothing else to be said. Yes, it was broad daylight in the middle of the day, but Ali has been waiting on this day to catch Gram slipping since he got out the hospital. It was already stuck in his mind to handle business on sight, fuck everything else. Deal with the consequences later. He has been riding thru Sprinkle every time he made a play or to go anywhere, he made sure that he was strapped but he was never able to catch his victim. He even went to some hole in the wall clubs over there on the late night, but could never saw Gram at Bonanza or Muds. By the time he came out the apartment he was very energized. Amped all the way up like he was on drugs.

Wheat and Hassan had a gold Chrysler Sebring crack rental and Ali told Wheat to let him drive. Once behind the wheel he pulled out his P89 Ruger loaded with 17 shots. "Damn I hate to have to throw this away on this fuck nigga" Ali says laughing and thinking how he will have to dump the gun after he catches this body. Riding thru Sprinkle he asked Wheat where did he see Gram at. Wheat was pointing Ali in directions all around the area to see if he could find him. Wheat let him know that he had on a black shirt and blue jeans. Wheat told Ali to swing around the block and go by Mets store. They circled around Aaron's brother car wash and then came back up Wood street. "There he goes coming out the store with some more Sprinkle boys" Wheat points him out.

"I got his ass now, Yo, Wheat pull your seat back and let your window down, I'm going to pull up and dump on his ass" Ali says Gram must have sensed the upcoming danger or he see death around the corner because he breaks off from the group and walks along the about 20 yards back from the road thru people yard headed back to Sprinkle. Ali turns off Wood street with nothing but murder on his mind. As soon as he gets his victim in good sight and range he hit the brakes and reaches over Wheat and let the P89 sing a song BAM! BAM! BAM! BAM! BAM! BAM! BAM! BAM!... He lets it rip the whole clip. He sees Gram slump to the ground and at the same time the rest of the group break out and run the opposite direction. He hits the gas and pulls off. He is trying to make it to Dash St. or Coleman Ave to Wheat sister house.

While turning at the light in front Whittaker school, Wheat tells Ali to pull over to Shell Rock girl house. They pull to the back of the house and Wheat ask for the straps and any work they have on them so that he could hide the work and gun before they try to make it across town. After he puts everything away he knocks on the backdoor to see who is home at the Alabama girls house. Shell Rock comes to the door and they all get out the car. They kick if for about 10 minutes and Ali ask Shell Rock to drive for them. Shell Rock is to the only one with a valid driver's license. Nobody mentions that they just did a drive by shooting that may have left someone dead. As they pull out to head towards C-Block they get blue lighted. The car is not stolen and Shell Rock has a driver's license and no drugs or weapons in the car, they figure they should be straight, "I know yall glad that I'm driving huh?" Shell Rock says. Little does he know how true that statement really is.

While waiting for the officer to come to the car, Shell Rock gets his license and the other papers for the car to give to the officer. The 4 to 5 other Orangeburg Sherriff dept. cruisers pull up with lights on. "This don't look like no regular traffic stop, what the fuck yall done did bo?" he asks with a confused look on his face. Ali, Wheat and Hassan all act as if they don't know what is really going on. Officer Sheppard (AKA Officer Friendly) approaches the car "All yall get the fuck out the car" once they all got out he asks where the owner to the car was at. It seems strange but everybody acts as if they were dumbfounded. Then Shell Rock ask what was the deal with all these cops for a traffic stop and officer Friendly lets them know that he dude that rented the car out beat the shit out of his wife because she would not give him any money to buy crack. That's a big relief to them. The officer lets them know they knew what was up with the car and the guy rented it out for crack and that he had to take the car back to the wife. He also let them know that he was going to let them go after he ran their names and if they didn't have any warrants he would let them leave. Ali and Hassan gave up fake names but Wheat gave up his government and it came back that he had warrants. Warrants for Home Invasion, Arm Robbery and Kidnapping!!!!!

CHAPTER 7
"IM BOUT THAT LIFE"

About 3 days later Jet walks in Sonya's apartment and says to Ali, "Gram out the hospital and he knows you and Wheat is the ones that shot him, he isn't going to the police but say he going to wait until you blow up and then get at you". Ali digests what Jet just said. Grams knows what it is and what it do. He doesn't want know beef or drama. Tell that nigga "I'm bout that life"

Wheat calls the apartment collect and Ali accepts the charges. "What's the verdict my nigga" Ali asks.

"Shit they got me for the move over there by Kick Booty we did". Ali is relieved that it was not for any moves with bodies tied to it but confused at the same time. He was confused because Wheat did not go inside on that mission. "You straight then because you weren't there, they don't have shit"

"They say they have got evidence"

"Evidence!!!??"

"They say they have my fingerprints on the dresser drawer in the house"

"Well you know that's a damn lie because you weren't there. All you got to do is sit for a minute then they will let you out, you know how that shit go." It gets quiet for a minute then Wheat tells Ali he needs to speak to him face to face and not over the phone. They kick it for the rest of the time remaining and Ali lets him know he will drop some money off and then come see him on his next visitation.

December 2002

Shit was going good for Ali, he had stacked 5 grand and had his re-up money. Going to Eutawville is paying off but it's an hour drive there and an hour coming back. Still everything is going smoothly.

"Ali, Wheat been calling here trying to catch up with you" Sonya tells him

"He says what he wants"

"He says he straight and got the money you sent him but he has not seen your ass yet". Ali kept putting off going down to the county to see Wheat but he made sure that his books stayed straight. He thought about it and said that he was going to do down there and check his dawg out Ali thinks to himself. "Have you seen Hassan" he asks Sonya.

"You know he stay with Lil C since his grandma put him out for stealing her credit card and buying all kind of shit with it". Ali just shook his head and was thinking about how he has not seen Hassan in a few days after he fronted him a half of ounce of crack.

New Year's Eve

"What they do" Ali ask Hassan when he saw him walk in the apartment with Jet and Chin.

"I got you Ali, I know it took a minute" Hassan says as he goes in his pocket and pulls out $200. Ali counts it and tell him that he is short on the count. "I know, I got you, I got some folks coming thru tonight when they money hit on the first"

"Yall niggas need to go to church tonight" Jet tells them

"I am not fucking with it, I'm not playing with the lord like that, in church one minute and then selling dope as soon as I leave" Ali lets Jet know.

"You can dedicate one night to the lord out the year, me and Shakira going tonight to bring the year in right" Jet says. Hassan and Chin agree to go but Ali declines.

Ali sits in the apartment and drink and catch plays to bring the new year in. That is his plan to do this year, get money and get fucked up. After Jet drops Chin and Hassan back at the apartment, Hassan gets Sonya to take him to his grandmother's house so that the can steal her car keys while she is sleep so he could go and collect his money. "You know I go to court in a few days, right?" Chin tells Ali while they sitting watching Court TV

"I thought you was supposed to go last month"

"They showed me the tape last month, but told me I have to plea this month or go to trial." Chin says. Ali says looking into the future "I'm going to be on top by the time you get out." After Sonya pulls up, Ali gets her car so he can make a few plays.

While on the Hilltop catching a few sales Ali's phone rings and he looks at the caller id and see that it is Sonya calling. "What up" he answers

"Come back to the apartment, I have to go get Hassan's grandma car before they tow it."

"What the fuck happen"

"They pull his ass for speeding and now they say he got warrants".

Ali finishes what he is doing and heads over to the apartment. He thinks that Hassan has warrants for the credit card thing.

CHAPTER 6
TIME TO MAN UP

JANUARY 1ST 2002

Ali was at his mom's crib in the country when he got the call from Sonya that he was waiting on. "You know that Hassan got Arm Robbery and receiving stolen goods charges?"

"How the fuck he get an arm robbery charge?"

"He said it's for CD and he got visit tomorrow and he wants to come holla at him and put some money on his books". Ali agrees that he will get down there as soon as possible. She asks him does he want her to come pick him up. He lets her know that Rashawn will be coming thru. He laid back on the bed pondering about how good shit was going and now everybody was getting locked up. A knock at the back door brought Ali out of his deep thoughts and he got up to let Rashawn in.

She comes in and headed straight to Ali's room as he waved to her parents leaving out the yard. "What's wrong with you" Ali asked her after seeing the expression on her face.

"I got something to tell you"

"Well go ahead and tell me"

"I'm pregnant"

"What you mean"

"I went to the doctor today and he said I'm pregnant"

"I thought you could not have any kids"

"I thought I could not either, my doctor said it has to be a miracle".

"So is it my baby".

"Don't play with me boy, hell yeah it's your baby". After that was said they had a discussion on what they would do next. Ali always wanted a child and he was going to take care of his seed and responsibility whenever the time came. It was time to man up

The next day Ali called his brother Sidney and asked him could he meet this kid name T.T. off 400 and show him how to get to his spot out in the country. Ali decided to buy a 1986 box Chevy with the bucket seats. Once they got to the country Ali paid T.T. 2 grand for the car and told Sidney he was going to the county jail to visit Wheat and Hassan. He decided to take the back way so he could flush the Chevy out to see what it could do and stop by Prince of Orange Mall so he could go to the music store to cop some cd's to put in his ride. When he got to the mall he got a few of Trick Daddy's cd's, www.thug.com, Chapter AK Verse 47, Thugs R Us and Thug Holiday, Project Pat's Mister Don't Play and 50 Cent's Get Rich or Die trying. Then he headed to Orangeburg Calhoun Detention Center. After putting a $100 each on Wheat and Hassan books he waited in line for them to be brought to the visitation area. Wheat was the first one to come up so he talked with him. "What they do?" Ali asks him as he sat down and picked up the phone.

"Just thugging thugga" Wheat responded.

"You have not seen Hassan back there?"

"No, they have him on the other side, I holla at him thru the door thou"

"So, what you talking about they have evidence?". Wheat went on to explain how he fucked up with the situation. After DB and Ali ran into some college boys trap spot that was jumping with weed, they forced the boys into the back room so they could keep an eye on them and then check the house for whatever stash they could find. It was Wheat job to stay on the porch and look out so no one could creep up on them with their backs turned. Now Wheat was telling Ali that he came in the house and was searching the front room while they were in the back. He didn't have any gloves on so when he touched the dresser he left his fingerprints. "So, what they saying"

"They talking about 25 years right now, 2 arm robberies and a home invasion." All Ali could do was shake his head at that one. "You know if they don't make it to court I can walk" Wheat said letting Ali know if the dudes came up missing, no witness or victims meant no case!

"My nigga I done been thru there and they done packed up and left, I tell you what, see if you can get some addresses and they will not make it". Ali put it out there that he would put in the work to get his dawg out. They talked a few more minutes until time was up and then they brought Hassan up.

"What they do" Ali asks

"Trying to see if these people give me a bond next week"

"So, what it looks like". Hassan then went on to give Ali the spill on what he was charged with and all kind of bullshit that didn't add up or make sense. They kicked it for the rest of the visit and Ali let him know that money was on his books and that he can call the apartment because he put money on the phone.

3 weeks later...

Ali was riding around with the music off listening to his car run. He just got the car dual exhaust with Flow Master pipes. His cell phone rings and he picks it up after he realizes it is Sonya. "What up"

"Wheat just called and said he needs to holla at you ASAP"

"Alright"

"I told him to call back in 30 minutes"

"I know he don't need no money, what he want"

"I'm going to let him tell you but you need to hear what he got to say". After she told him that he hung up and headed towards he apartment. He was wondering what he needed to talk to him about asap.

About 5 minutes after he arrived at the apartment he got the phone call. "What they do" he said after he accepted the call.

"That fuck nigga Hassan done sign statements on me!"

"WHAT!!!!"

"They just served me with 5 new warrants today, 2 arm robberies, 2 kidnappings, and home invasions, and they say they going to get some more warrants."

"Damn, why you say Hassan wrote statements"

"Because it says right here on the warrant that defendant Hassan Gamble wrote statements the he and Codefendant John Sharks committed arm robbery......" Wheat went on to explain that all the warrants started off saying the same thing and that was Hassan implicated him.

"You see the nigga yet"

"I holla at him thru the door and let him know what was up and he ain't come back to the door since".

Ali then asked Sonya who was looking at him when the last time Hassan called to the house. She told him the day before. "You think that nigga hit everybody up?"

"Shit, more than likely, he didn't spare me". The phone let them know that they their time was almost up. Ali told Wheat to hold his head and that he would get at DB and Lil C and let them know the latest news.

MARCH 2003...

Ali and Rashawn was on the way back from Eutawville to Orangeburg when they got pulled over. "Shit, I got to hide this work" Ali said as he stuck the cookie of crack and ounce of coke under his nuts and got the paperwork out of the glove compartment and Chin's driver's license out of his pocket. The officer came to the car and let Ali know he was speeding and he was going to run his name and give him a ticket and send them on their way. Ali had Chin's license since he turned himself in to do some time on a drug charge but what he didn't realize was that as soon as you get sentenced they automatically suspends your license. The officer got the report back that the license was suspended but also got a call from Orangeburg Narcotics division that he knew for sure that Chin was locked up. So, the officer gets out the car and asks Ali to step out of his vehicle. He searched him and then put him in cuffs and sat him in the back seat of the police cruiser. The officer got a female to search her. After that he came back to the cruiser and let him know that he knew his real name was Adrian Haggard. The officer got in front and ran his name and let him know if he didn't have any other warrants he would let him go with a ticket. A few seconds he hears the officer say "What the hell" to himself. Then he turns around after saying he has the suspect in custody and will transport him to the county jail. Ali looked bewildered and asks "I thought you was going to let me go and let my girl drive?"

"Yeah that was before I knew you had all them arm robberies and home invasions!!!"

CHAPTER 7
"I TAKE MINE, STRAIGHT UP WITH NO CHASE"

ORANGEBURG CALHOUN DETENTION CENTER...

"You will not be seeing the streets for a long-time Mr. Haggard" the detective tells Ali.

"What the fuck you mean?"

"Look at these" the detective said as he passed the warrants to Ali. As he reads the warrants he gets a sick feeling in his stomach and light headed. They read the same things that Wheat told him his stated. Ali was now charged with the arm robbery of Craig Dixon. He couldn't believe that Hassan put him in this bullshit. The detective asks him did he want a cigarette because this was going to be the last one that he would get in a very long time. He told him no because he didn't smoke but he did need something to get his mind right. Then the detective asked would he like to make a statement and Ali told him "When I drink, I take mine straight up with no chase" and asked to be taking the back.

Ali was taken to B Pod and when he got thru the doors he could hear Wheat screaming from behind a lock cell door. "Nigga what they do" Wheat screams.

"That nigga hit me up too"

"I told you that nigga wasn't right"

"I'm about to get put in your cell" Ali said and went to the booth and asked to be placed in the same cell with his comrade. When he walked in the cell he sees two thick manila envelopes on the desk. "What the fuck is that" he asks.

"Our Discovery" (Evidence)

They both stayed up all night going over the evidence against them. Ali was amazed at how the shit went down to get them locked up. The robbery of Craig Dixon went as this.

'Two masked men kicked the door open of the mobile home that Craig's girlfriend stayed in and once they made entry they located Craig and his girlfriend in the master bedroom. After pointing firearms at the victims and demanding drugs and money and the victims explaining they didn't have any of either. The two suspects decided to take victim #1 (Craig Dixon) to his mother's residence to retrieve his money and drug stash. The smaller of the two suspects calls someone on his cellphone and tells them to come and watch the second victim while they take the 1st victim to the mother's house. Victim #2 could see thru the blinds of her bedroom window that a tan colored Honda pulls up and drop someone off and pulls off. After being tied up and placed on the bed on her stomach, Suspect #1 and #2 takes victim #1 out and places him in the car. Victim #2 states that while being held at gunpoint by the 3rd suspect he took off all her jewelry. Also, while she was held hostage Suspect #3 continually stuck his finder inside her virgina. Ali and Wheat shook their head at what Hassan did. "I told you that nigga was a freak" Wheat said to Ali

"I'm just glad we don't have a rape charge". Ali said.

Both statements stated that they could not identify any of the suspects because they wore masks and could not recall any of the voices. What put them on to the suspects as the perpetrators was a follow up interview with the victims and the victims stating that they heard it was the Dash Street Posse that did it. They also let the detectives know that Hassan's sister drove a car similar to the one the victim saw that night. They gave a list of Ali, Wheat and Hassan as possible suspects. Hassan name came up on a list at Woody's Pawn Shop for pawning some jewelry. Come to find out Hassan did the most stupidest thing you could ever do and that was pawn the jewelry with his own I.D.??!!!?? After getting arrested he told them what they wanted to hear.

"The only thing they have on us is these statements" Ali tells Wheat.

"And they believing everything he is saying too"

"I'm going to holla at that nigga in the morning"

The next morning Ali went to the door that separated A-Pod and B-Pod and got Hassan to come and talk to him.

"What the fucks up my nigga"

"Ali, they tricked me and got me to say all that shit"

"These folks trying to give me 30 years behind this shit"

"I was just trying to get a bond and dip back up north and not come back"

"You got me fucked up with this bullshit and I got a baby on the way"

"I heard"

"What you going to do"

"Whatever you need me to do".

Ali ran down the plan he had to get them out the situation they were in. Ali was going to get a lawyer and private investigator and Hassan would write a new statement that said he lied and was pressured into saying what he said on the first ones. With no positive id of any of the suspects the worst charge Hassan could get is the receiving stolen goods.

The next day Ali called Sonya to go take the money she had of his to get a lawyer named Virgin Johnson and she did and everything worked out as planned. Ali and Lil C was taken to General Sessions to get bonds because a magistrate Judge couldn't set bonds on those serious charges. After all the evidence was presented they was given $25,000 surety bonds. The process took about 2 months and damn near broke Ali. He always said that freedom was priceless. He would go broke not to spend another day in jail.

CHAPTER 8
FREEDOM IS PRICELESS

"Thanks for taking care of that for me" Ali tells Sonya after the bondsman drops him off to her apartment. Ali always knew that freedom was priceless.

"No problem, any time you need me I'm there"

"So, what has been going on since I been gone". Sonya went on to tell Ali what was the deal. She was telling him that Jet was the only one that be over there most of the time. Sometimes Aaron be over there but Jet say that he just trying to catch his sales because he falling off.

Ali went to Sidney's house to get his car that he had since he was locked up. Now that Ali was home Sidney was locked up on a bench warrant in Lexington County. When he got there, he saw that his god brother copped him a money green 320 Mercedes Benz. When he saw that and he said that he really had to step his game up. After he got back to Sonya's apartment, Karen was there in the living room with some tight ass dickies on that hugged her ass like a glove. Karen was trying to cop some work from Jet but he was out and waiting on his boss man Kool Keith (Aaron's older brother) to re-up. Karen is Aaron and Kool Keith sister, so she had checked with her brother and knew that he was out but was hoping that Jet had something. Jet let her know that Ali may have something and she asked Ali and he let her know that he had an ounce on him. It was the same ounce that he went to jail with a few months ago, Karen asked Ali how much would he let it go for in that little girl voice of hers. "Stack" Ali said letting her know that he wanted a grand for it. She agreed on the price and pulled out a big wad of money and counted out a thousand dollars. While she was counting the money out Jet couldn't help but hate and talk slick and said "You know that ain't that bling that I be having". She told Jet that she had to get something and that she didn't know when her brother would be straight. She told Ali that she was going to need more because it would not last that long on the block because she was the only one that had any work over there. Ali gave her his cell number and let her know he would be good later.

Ali jumped in his car to head down to Eutawville to holla at Twan C to get right. When Ali got down there he copped a zone of hard and a half of soft. Ali wasn't back in Orangeburg a good 2 hours and Karen called him. "You think you can bring me a half by my mama house".

"I'm on the way". Ali stopped on Dash St and weighed out 14 grams on the scale and jumped in the Chevy and headed over to Sprinkle. On the way over he checked and made sure he had one in the head of the Glock 357 with the 10-round clip. Ali was going back to the same house and yard when he got jumped that night. Ali wasn't going to get caught slipping ever again, he had to get that money because it was money over everything. That was what he was on.

As Ali pulling up he was calling Karen back to let her know he was outside. Karen came out with some daisy dukes, coochie cutter shorts on showing off her pretty ass legs. As she walked to the car she had to reach down and pull her shorts down some because her fat ass and pussy kept eating them up. "I thought you wasn't going to come" She said once she made it to the driver side of the car.

"Why you say that"

"Because you got into it with Lo-Lo and Gram the last time you been over here"

"Fuck them niggas, you want this half? Matter of fact where Gram ass at anyway" Ali said then becoming aware of his surroundings at the same time reaching for his strap

"That boy don't want no problems, he the one that told me to call you to get some work, you know he don't want to buy from you so he buys it from me"

"What he trying to get?

"Half of slab, what you think they call him gram for" at that they both laughed. Karen pulled out the money and handed it to him and he gave her the half, Ali was about to put the money in his pocket and she said "That's $450 right there"

"Hold a minute, my half go for $500"

"Let me get it for $450" She says with that sweet little girl voice.

"Nope, let me get my $50". They go back and forth for about 5 minutes on the price and she ended up sweet talking him and get it for the 450 with a promise to call back and get more later.

Ali ran out all the crack he had and had to ride all the way back to see Twan C to re-up. Ali felt good that he moved all the work that day, although Karen copped most of it in weight, he still made a profit. He let all the niggas he was fucking with know that he was back in business.

With Black Bikers week coming up in a few weeks in Myrtle Beach and then C-Lo coming home about a week or so later, Ali felt like things was looking good for him. Karen was still copping work from Ali from time to time whenever Jet and Kev was out. Karen kept complaining that the crack was not all that and that her customers was talking shit. So she wouldn't buy no more than a half when she copped from him. Ali always thought that one monkey didn't stop no show.

Ali was on Dash Street at the Thomas boys house and Jaylin came thru. Jaylin grew up on the block also but was a straight square, sponge bob type nigga. He wanted to holla at him about his cousin Fat Boy who wanted to get at Ali and fuck with him on the work tip. Fat Boy heard all about how Ali was getting rid of all the dope around there and knew that he would bust his gun if he had too but was all about getting money now.

Ali knew Fat Boy good because he was off Dash Street and was older than he was but was getting money in other cities. Ali remembered when Juvenile came out with the song 400 Degrees and said on a verse "see that 98 Mercedes on tv, I bought that" that Fat Boy had a big body 500 SEL sitting on some chrome Lion Hart 18' rims. Fat Boy was eating really good and Ali knew it and could see himself coming up fucking with him. So, he agreed to meet up with Fat Boy and see what he was talking about.

CHAPTER 9
"BOX CHEVY SHAKING"

When Ali and Fat Boy met up at Fat Boy pops trailer on Dash St, shit went alright. Ali let him know what he could do and Fat Boy let Ali know that he had work for days and never ran out. The only thing was Fat Boy wanted $900 a zone. Ali told him that he could get a better price at $750 but Fat Boy said "I got the best shit around here" arrogantly. He also let Ali know that he would front him the work and he could just sit back and stack his paper. All of Fat Boy ounces no matter what weighed 27 grams. They agreed on a price of $850 a zone. Before he left Fat Boy said with a up north accent "Yo, I'm telling you that they going to be calling you back for more, and you don't have to give up that much. 6 grams is a quarter of this straight drop". Ali calculated the numbers and liked what he came up with, he could get a stack for 24 grams.

Ali had the Box Chevy shaking all around town getting rid of the work. Everybody was loving the new dope. Only some complained about the size of it but never the quality of it. He had that good shit. Karen even said the smokers think it's the same shit she normally has so she became a regular customer.

"What's up Sonya" Ali asks as he is sitting down on her couch eating Bojangles chicken.

"About to go up and see C-lo tomorrow"

"I know that nigga happy he about to get out soon"

"Yeah, he is very excited" she said sadly

"What they fuck wrong with you"

"He doesn't want me to go to Bike Week". Ali laughs and tell her too bad and he will have fun for the both of them. Sonya gets up and goes in her room crying because she is emotional like that. Ali feels bad so he goes to their room to cheer her up and tell her he will bring her something back. That helps a little bit and she comes back to the living room. Sonya then tells him that Karen be talking about him when she comes over there and she thinks that Karen wants to give him some pussy. Ali likes the sound of that and can imagine himself playing in that pussy. Sonya lets him know that she Karen still fucking Jet also and that she is the reason that Jet and Tech 9 don't talk to each other no more so he better watch out and be careful. He thought about it and couldn't see how two homeboys who was tight as thieves could fall out about some pussy, some young pussy at that and they both have fine ass girls at home? Ali knows that he cannot trust a big butt and a smile.

BIKE WEEK 2003

Ali is riding down the strip bumping JT Money's Blood, Sweat and Years cd. Ali and two of the Thomas brothers are just riding around bike week looking at the females and all the tight whips the niggas done tricked out. When they tried to holla at all the hoes, sack chasers and foot draggers they couldn't get no play because they did not have a paint job or rims on their car. When Ali went to holla at a petite red bone and she just looked and passed him to go to a Chevy that was painted and on rims. "Fuck that shit, when I get back to the city I'm going to get me some rims." Ali told the Thomas brothers.

"You know they say that a new paint job will get you a blow job" Mitch said and they all laughed at that

Ali and the Thomas boys ended up at Jet's room on Ocean Blvd. Jet and Big Nose was in there rolling up some mid. They all kicked it for a minute and Ali decided to he was going to walk the strip. While walking down the strip he was taking pictures of every bad bitch that he saw so that he could send to his niggas behind the wall. He would stop and ask could he take a picture for his niggas that's locked up and they would just bust it open for him. As he made it down the strip he spots Sonya and Karen on the other side of the street so he decides to go over and fuck with them.

"Ohhhh, I'm going to tell" Ali says as he walks up on Sonya.

"So, I am not doing nothing" she responds. Ali and Karen laugh for a second and then Karen ask Ali will he take a picture with him using his government name when she speaks but with that sweet little voice she has he went along and says yes. Karen gives Sonya a camera and asks her to take some pictures of her and Ali. She gets in front of him and grinds that fat ass on his crouch. Ali quickly gets a hard on before the picture is taken. Karen knows already that Ali likes what he sees and feels because his little man is pressing hard on her ass. After taking a few photos in different positions. Karen ask did he have a room and he said he didn't but said he was thinking about getting one. Ali and Karen could feel the chemistry in the air so they decided to get a room to chill for the night. But after trying a few hotels and finding out that everything was booked they figured it wasn't meant to be but planned to get up when they got back to the city.

Chapter 10
Good Pussy

Once back in Orangeburg, Ali gets the phone call he was waiting on. "What's on your mind?" He says when he answers

"You" Karen responds

"Me"

"Yeah you"

"Well I'm making a few rounds to get some of this money I spent and missed while I was in down at the beach?"

"I thought we was supposed to get up once we got back?" Karen says getting straight to the point. That was like music to Ali's ears. "Well I'm getting a room later on tonight, you going to show up?" he said to her.

"I already got a room and I got you something to drink"

"Where at?"

"Southern Lodge on 601, I'm in the suite". All Ali could think of was getting all up in her. So he decided to cut everything else short and get some pussy instead of chasing some lost paper.

When he got to the room all he could think about was he was finally about to find out what the fuss was about behind that pussy. Ali wondered was it worth losing a friend over. He didn't know but he was sure about to find out he thought with a smile on his face. When Karen opened the door all he could say was "Damn!". Karen had on a matching red and black silk panty and bra set. She looked like a dark skin version of the rapper Trina. Everything on her was nice and tight and you could not tell that she had had a baby. He walked into the room and stood by the TV Karen fixed a drink and passed it to him and he could tell that she was feeling really good.

After talking and kicking it for about 10-15 minutes and Ali was on his second drink she told him to take off his clothes. She got up and turned on a radio she brought with a cd just for the night. The first song she played was perfect for the strip show she put on. She played Petey Pablo's "Freak a Leak" and she was putting on like she was on a stage in a strip club. When she crawled up on the bed where Ali was she could tell he was ready because his dick was trying its best to escape his boxers. Karen took over from there. She started taking his boxers off and then she grabbed his dick and took her tongue and started licking the head and putting the tip of her tongue in the pee hole. Then she started giving some of the best head he ever had. He felt himself about to come but couldn't open his mouth to say a word. Karen must have known that also because she stopped and said "No you not, you going to give me some of this good dick first, I just wanted to see how you taste." She took off her panties and climbed on top of Ali and gave him a rodeo ride to remember. Her mixed cd was playing some music that was turning them both on. For about 15 minutes she was doing her thing and asking the whole time was it good to him. Then she rolled off top of him and told Ali "It's your turn, I want you to fuck me now" as she opened her legs for him to enter. He enters her and begin to put his pound game down. Karen is moaning and groaning and screaming he was killing her and that was making him go even harder. The pussy was on 1000, he didn't know if she was close built or haven't had sex in a while but the pussy fit his dick like a glove. He didn't last a full 10 minutes before he busted off inside her. Yes, it's official, she got some bomb ass pussy he says to himself.

While still in bed after their second-round Karen hits Ali with a question way out in left field. "Adrian, you going to be my boyfriend?" in that soft voice of hers.

"I am not with the girlfriend thing but we can kick it thou" he lets her know. She seemed to be alright with that and just got closer to him and went under the cover and started sucking on Ali softness but quickly gets it to get back hard. Her phone rings in between deep throat sucks and she gets up to answer the phone. She then turns around and asks him is he straight and he lets her know that he was and she let the caller know that she would bring it. After she got off the phone she explained that when she leaves off the block she gives her mother some work to keep things going while she is gone.

When they get on Sprinkle to her mother's house she asks to hold the scale so she can cut the dope up. Before she gets out the car she leans over and gives Ali a kiss straight in the mouth. So whoever was out there now knew that they was fucking.

CHAPTER 11
DADDY'S PRINCESS

The next week was a good week for Ali. Rashawn gave birth to his first seed. A baby girl and he went out and treated himself to becoming a father by buying some 20 inch spokes to put on his box Chevy. You couldn't tell Ali shit because he felt good about himself. He also knew that his homie would be home the following week.

"What they do my nigga" Ali ask C-Lo while dapping him up. And as with every time when either one goes to jail or they don't see each other for a while they go to wrestling to see who can get who. It starts off by aggressively pushing each other in the chest, what would look like to somebody who does not know any better would think they was serious. C-Lo who has been working out for the past year gets the best of Ali and slams him to the ground.

Afterwards, Ali and C-Lo sat down and talked about what all is going on around the "Dirty Burg". Ali lets him know that them together they can get shit to jumping. He also lets him know the he can get some good deals from Fat Boy who he is fucking with or he could stick with his brother. Ali gives him 7 grams hard and 7 grams soft as a coming home present and told him he would take him out that weekend.

"I see you trying to stunt on me with them twinkies" C-Lo says.

"You know I was going to get at ya, I was going to go broke just to stunt on you" Ali says and they laugh. Ali hit his stash up real hard by buying those rims and everything for his daughter that was just born. He wasn't tripping because he knew that he would get it back and double.

After Ali left C-Lo crib so that he could get himself together with the home front. He pulled up to the Bojangles gas station and ran into Pretty. Pretty was a nigga from Miami that had been in Orangeburg for a few years now. A real life gutter nigga. He gets money but will also pull a move on you. He had already robbed a few niggas in the city and it was rumored that he was up there because he had robbed so many niggas down there in Miami. They met while they were in the county jail. Both of them had arm robberies and home invasion charges at the time. Pretty was in there for a home invasion on this nigga named Bob Cat from Santee. They respected each other gangsta. "What's up my nigga?" Pretty asks Ali

"It's nothing fool"

"I heard that boy C-Lo got out today?"

"Yeah, he home I just left his spot"

"Tell that nigga I said come by my house and holla at me, I got something for him"

"Alright, I will do that."

The next day when Ali got to C-Lo's apartment he let him know what Pretty said and they decided to go over to Pretty's trap in country colony. They both jumped in their whips and headed over there. C-Lo still had his 1984 Fleetwood Caddy with the 17 inch spokes. When they got to Pretty's spot they got out their cars and greeted Pretty with daps. Then Pretty went on to tell them that he had the zones for $700 a piece and to fuck with him. That was the best price around town. C-lo let him know that he was going to fuck with him when he got his money right but Pretty went and got C-Lo a zone of soft and hard and told him to bring him $1400 back. Pretty then asked Ali what he wanted to do and Ali said he would fuck with him and Pretty pulled the same thing out that he gave to C-Lo as if he knew Ali would accept. With that, Ali had yet another plug to get work from.

CHAPTER 12
WHEN YOU LOVE THE STREETS, THE STREETS LOVE YOU BACK

JUNE 2003

Ali was sitting back just thinking about how everything was coming together. Now he had his right-hand man back and they were getting paid together. Ali was fucking with Fat Boy, Pretty, Sidney and Twan C when he needed work. Even though he was only getting like 2 ounces at a time, he was getting rid of the shit real fast.

He was fucking with Karen heavy now and he was even staying over to her house on Sprinkle some nights. He never went over there without being strapped so he didn't give a fuck about what a nigga had to say. He felt like Karen was his bitch now and he could go and come as he pleased.

Jet ended up giving C-Lo a set of dubs off one of his Chevy's so now he and Ali was riding big. Ali pulled up to C-Lo's apartment and went inside. They were inside talking about their cousin O-Zone that was about to come home from federal prison. O-Zone was a real money go getter. Ali remembered reading about him in the newspaper back in 95-96. O-Zone got hit with 2 keys of crack and over 60 grand cash in the Holiday Inn on John C. Calhoun Drive. He ended up going fed and took them white folks to trial. AND HE BEAT THEM!!! That was the only person that Ali knew that took the feds to trial and won. They ended up hitting O-Zone with a jury tampering charge because he tried to bribe the jury for a not guilty verdict. He got his name for his talents on the football field. He was the starting quarterback for South Carolina State University and signed a deal with that new expansion NFL team the Carolina Panthers. He took the signing bonus and brought a shopping plaza down in Miami but being the hood nigga that he was he still loved the streets because that's what he did best.

"we going to throw him a coming home party when he gets out" Jet was telling everybody. Jet wanted to show his big cuz that lil cuz was getting money now. Jet planned to throw the party on the block in the Ritz parking lot.

"Damn this shit is packed" Ali says as he pulls up in the Ritz parking lot. Old school niggas and bitches came out to show O-Zone love. When you love the streets, the streets love you back. Ali sat back and thought that he wanted to get love like that. He thought that the next year on his bday he was going to do it big just like that. He gave O-Zone a $100 and said welcome home when he made it over to where he was at. Everybody ate and got fucked up and was telling stories of what they knew about O-Zone. Fat Boy was holding the floor telling stories about how O-Zone use to stunt back in the days. Ali ended up talking to O and telling him that he heard a lot about him and wanted to get up with him so they could talk more. O-Zone could see the hunger in Ali's young eyes and told him to come by the house anytime to talk.

About a week later Ali was on Dash St. making a play and was circling the block and saw O-Zone walking out his house with a gray sweat suit on in the middle of summer. He laughed to himself and thought that O-Zone was really burnt out from doing that time. He pulled over and got out and went to holla at him. What started off as a brief conversation ended up a 3-hour talk. As Ali was about to leave a black Dodge Intrepid pulled up. Thinking it was the jump out boys, Ali prepared himself to run. Ali was strapped and had work on him. He was relieved when Suave jumped out the car. "What they do?" Ali smiled and dapped him up, O-Zone came off the porch and said "I know that's not pretty boy Suave?". Then it was like a small family reunion. Suave and O-Zone use to get money together back in the early 90's. They sat and talked for another 2 hrs. Before it was all said and done, O-Zone let Ali know that shit was about to get on and popping. He still had connects from back in the day that wanted to get things back to the way it used to be.

Chapter 13
"I Keep It Clean"

True to his word, O-Zone got the sack again and was letting it do what it do.
"What's up O" Ali says

"Nothing but the price of pussy"

"I got like $3,500"

"Shit, you can get a Big 8 for that"

"That's what it is then" Ali said as he counts the money out and hands it to O-Zone. Ali had been fucking with him since he let him know he had it. They were at O-Zone spot on State Court and he came from the back room with a chunk of coke that looked like it came straight off the brick. Ali looked at it after he got it and was like 'DAMN!!!'. He could see the flakes and the shine in the rock. It was dark brown but had the shine of fish scale. O-Zone could see that he is amazed with what he sees so he tells him "I don't fuck with my shit, I keep it clean". With that move right there, they both knew that Ali was locked in.

Ali gets the coke and take it to Pretty's trap in Country Colony. Pretty was a beast with the whip game. He could easily whip one ounce into two. Since Ali was fucking with Pretty, he told him that he would cook dope for him whenever he wanted crack. Pretty could see how Ali and C-Lo was moving work thru the city. He personally sold them about 2-3 keys in a month, ounce by ounce. He came up so much off them the he had to drop a jewel on them. "Look my nigga, don't ever buy crack, buy coke and cook it yourself" he told them one day. He saw that Ali and C-Lo was about to take over the city and he didn't want nobody else to rape them as he did with the work. He didn't have any work so he had to shop locally to grab something. He did have a cousin from Miami that use to hit him with work but that stopped. Ali knew what it was, Pretty had fucked the money up or fucked his peeps out the work.

"What this look like?" Ali asks Pretty as he showed him the work that he just got.

"This shit looks good, but that don't mean shit" Pretty said and went on to explain that some niggas recompress their cocaine which is they take some pure cocaine and mix it with cut and then put it back together. He also confirmed what Ali had figured out and that was he jammed his cousin out of some work because he started sending him re-rock. While he was talking, he was cooking the work. He dropped 21 grams and went to whipping. He kept telling Ali to dump table spoons of hot water in the beaker because the dope was soaking up the water. "This shit look like some oil base" he said while beating the coke like it stole something. After he sat the beaker down and the cookie got hard they watched the numbers on the scale as the swollen cookie did what it do. The scale read 51.3 grams!!! "That's that shit right there" was all he could say as he shook his head. He let Ali know that they needed to get as much of that work as they could. O-Zone had super clean work and oil base at that. Oil base dope was the best dope they could have because they were whipping and stretching everything.

Ali was really making moves now that he had some A-1 work. He was seeing 0-Zone at least once a day. One day while he was copping, O-Zone gave him something to think about. "You got bond and lawyer money put up". Ali wasn't even thinking like that. All he was doing was making quick flips and buy clothes, shoes, jewelry and pussy. And to top it off he was partying every day of the week. He thought about it and then asked what he thought was a good number to have for that.

"At least 10 stacks, with a state charge $2,500-$5,000 for a lawyer and the same thing for the bond and then on top of that you need to have your re-up money". O-Zone said and Ali thought that he had to do that.

Ali was on a mission to get money, he gave Rashawn 3 stacks to put up for their daughter, had about 8 stacks in the stash and had his reup money. O-

Zone let him know that when he got to a half a key that he would let him get it for 13 racks.

Karen was still brining Ali a lot of the money off Sprinkle and they were fucking around real heavy. It got so intense that he asked her to get an apartment for them. She was happy and excited so she agreed to do it. They were at their favorite hotel Ramada Inn, that way they were close when her mother needed to reup. She went under the covers and took Ali in her mouth and he couldn't believe how good life was. He had money, bitches and a car. Karen sex game was top notch. She treated his dick like it was her personal toy. She gave him head until she felt he was about to come and like always she got off and jumped on the dick and rode him until he came inside of her.

The next day Karen let Ali know that she found an apartment in the same complex as Sonya and C-Lo and that her aunt was going to put it in her name. "You know that your brothers are not coming to our spot" He let her know. They had a small argument about the fact Ali didn't fuck with or trust her brothers. That always caused problems in their relationship. Ali couldn't see why Karen didn't see things his way. Hell, it was her that came back and told him all the hating and shit talking that her brothers did. Like they didn't know why she was fucking with him and that he was broke all kind of other shit about the dope he be selling. He always tells her that they only claim her now because she is getting money but before then she was treated just like a step child. He got tired of the bullshit and the fact that she couldn't see in the future. They kind of ended it that day but she would see later what he was talking about. She even went as far as getting Ali's government named tattooed on her neck because she said that he was the realest nigga that she ever fucked with!

OCTOBER 2003

Just as things were at its best, Ali had 10 stacks put away for bond and lawyer, and over 13 stacks to buy a half a key. He got an apartment on Baugh street for him and Rashawn and the baby and had about 10 stacks to blow. He had been trying to call O-Zone for a few days now and could not catch up with him. So he was grabbing work off Whoodie and Fat Boy to get him by until O-Zone resurfaced. It wasn't strange to Ali because O-Zone would disappear for a day or so when he went to re-up but it had been about a week now?

C-Lo had hooked Ali up with Whoodie when he couldn't get nothing. One day they pulled up to Whoodie daddy's house on Solomon Terrace and immediately he started talking shit. "Yeah lil nigga, you got to buy dope from me now since your boy locked up". Ali got a strange look on his face because he did not know what he was talking about. He went on to tell them that O-Zone was locked up again and this time he got caught with 2 bricks coming out of the "A" (Atlanta, Ga). Ali did not know what he was going to do now. He had his money up or so he thought at the time. Going thru Whoodie or Fat Boy was tough because the numbers was fucked up and they played with the work.

With Homecoming falling in November this year, Ali decided he was going to ball out. C-Lo was putting the caddy in the shop and was putting 20' spinners on his ride. So Ali decided he had to stunt on his dawg. He went and copped a 2000 Ford Crown Victoria, it was royal blue with a red stripe down the side. He then ordered some 22' inch spinners and put the car in the shop to get a few clear coats sprayed on it. All in one week

Homecoming Day Ali and C-Lo showed out for the city. They let everybody know that the Dash Street Boys was getting money. They decided to hit club Shorty's up first. When they hit the parking lot they knew they were on top of their game. It was all eyes on them. In just a year, Ali had bounced all the way back and was eating really good. A few people had to ask did his rims have a remote on them because they had been stopped over 10 minutes and they were still spinning. Inside the club, Ali went and brought two bottles of Moet for him and his dawg. That night was the first night for a lot of things. First time he brought Moet, the first time he popped ecstasy and the first time he saw Isis. She was a bad little bitch. Light skin, pretty face and long hair. She didn't have the fat ass like he preferred but she did have a lil bump back there. "Damn, I want to fuck that bitch right there" Ali tells C-Lo and points her out. C-lo then lets him know that is Aaron's girlfriend and she is pregnant by him. He didn't like the sound of her being pregnant so he took his mind off her.

"Let's put our money together and get a whole brick" Ali told C-Lo. What Ali didn't know was that C-Lo was fucking all his money up and not saving.

"I'm straight, you buy your own shit and I buy mine"

"Well I'm going to get me a half of block in the morning". They finished partying hard that night and Ali found out that Moet and X went well together.

"Got damn Fat Boy, let a nigga get a half of block clean". Ali was trying to get Fat Boy to sell him a half of key not stepped on but Fat Boy had other plans. He was trying to tell Ali that his shit was clean but Ali knew better.

"Who use to sell you clean work in the Burg" Fat Boy wanted to know

"O-Zone, give it to a nigga straight off the brick" Ali let him know

Fat Boy started going on and on about how O-Zone back doored him and went to his peeps down in the "A". Sounded like the same shit Whoodie was saying. In the end, Ali, did get a half of brick but it wasn't what Ali expected. It was 18 single ounces and each ounce was weighing 27 grams and the price tag was 14 stacks!!! 'That fat ass nigga know he can drag a muther fucker but that's all good because when I find another plug I am not fucking with his fat ass no more' Ali thought.

CHAPTER 14
NIGGAS SHAKING AND FAKING

Ali saw the new year as more time to get more money. Ali sat back and thought about less than 2 years ago, he was broke and fucked up. Now at 22 years old he was getting real paper or so he thought. He had his bond and lawyer money and over 30 stacks to work with so he thought that he would get his first brick.

He got his money and counted out 24 racks and went to cop his first brick. He wanted to stunt and let niggas know that he had his money right. Ali jumped in the Crown Vic and sped over to Aaron St. He went to holla at Jet to see if he could holla at his boss man and get him a brick. Jet went on Sprinkle to Kool Keith's momma house and tried to see what was up. He couldn't come up with nothing but let him know that he had a few ounces for sale already cooked up. Ali leaves off Aaron St. and heads over to Country Colony to see if Pretty could come up with something and he couldn't do anything. He then goes up to his brother Sidney's spot and he is on "E" also. He left there and went on C-Block and that was a no go and they had only a few Big 8's. Ali ended up going to every heavy hitter in the city or who he thought was a heavy hitter and nobody could come up with a brick. The way they be flawging in the city he thought that niggas was bossed up and caked up. Ali even broke down and went to Fat Boy but he said he had it but couldn't sell it to him like that. Ali got tired of all the running around and just grabbed a half of block off Fat Boy.

The first part of February Ali was sitting on about 40 stacks. 'Fuck it, I'm about to go buy me a toy' Ali says to himself. He always said when he got his money right he was going to buy himself a big boy truck so that's what he went out shopping for. He saw a 2001 whit Ford Expedition Eddie Bauer edition. Over 20 stacks later and some paperwork, Rashawn was driving off the lot in the expo.

Later that night Ali wanted to hit Columbia and party a lil bit. At the club Main Event he ran into an old schoolmate named Doobie that was throwing parties. Doobie was telling Ali that he been hearing his name all the way in the Metro and that he needed to get into throwing parties because it was some good money in that. Ali was wondering how a square like him knew what was going on in the streets. But the next words that came out of his mouth was like music to his ears.

"You remember Nick Williams that we use to go to school with, he lives in the 'A' now".

That was all that Ali needed to hear. Nick's sister was married to a brick mason from what they streets was saying. She was fucking with this nigga named Gizmo who was originally from New York but migrated down south to the 'Dirty Burg'. Rumor has it that Gizmo use to smoke crack up north but he kicked that habit and got a bigger and better habit "Getting Money". If the street talk was correct then Ali knew Gizmo was going to be his next plug. Before the night was over with Ali made sure that Doobie would get in contact with Nick and let him know that he needed to holla at him.

About a week later Ali got the call he was waiting for.

"Who dis"

"Nick"

"What they do player"

"Trying to see what's up with you"

"I am not trying to talk over the phone but I will make it worth it if you come holla at the kid"

"I don't fuck around with no bullshit"

"And I am not no bullshit ass nigga either"

"I will be down there tomorrow"

The next night Ali was sitting in the McDonalds parking lot on the corner of Hwy 601 and John C Calhoun, his phone rings. "Yo"

"Where you at"

"Where I said I was going to be"

"What you in"

"The biggest thing in the parking lot" Ali says with a smirk. Nick pulls up next to Ali and jumped out of his car and hopped in the truck with Ali and says "Oh you doing it like that"

"Just like that"

"So what you talking about"

"I'm trying to get a whole one"

Nick had to sit and think about what was all going on. He knew Ali from school and knew that he was a wild ass nigga. Ali was known to rob niggas and take niggas shit. Ali also knew what Nick could have been thinking and knew about his past, so he was prepared for that. He reached in the center console of his truck and pulled out a plastic BI-LO bag and handed it to Nick.

"What's that"

"23"

"Well I got to go to the 'A' and get it"

"Just take that with you and bring my shit back"

"You just going to give me your money like that". Nick says and Ali knew it was his time to shine and stunt.

"It's plenty more where that came from, I'm caked up now, plus I know where your momma stay at"

"Alright, I'm going to go down and grab it and come back up" Nick says before he gets out the truck he looks back and tell Ali not to drive his truck no more with them big ass rims on there. Ali knew what they lick was. Nick didn't trust Ali like that, he knew the work was closer than the 'A' because Gizmo was serving niggas all over the Carolina's.

The next day Nick pulled up to Ali's apartment on Baugh St. in a blue ford astro minivan. "Nick, you think you a soccer dad or something" and they both started laughing. Nick handed Ali the same BI-LO bag with a brick wrapped in a t-shirt. Nick told Ali that if he ever needed something to holla at him and that Gizmo said he couldn't do it for the 23 no more he had to have 24.

CHAPTER 15
FROM A NICK TO A BRICK

Ali went back in the apartment and was glad Rashawn was at work and the baby was with her parents. He sat there for about 10 minutes in the living room looking at the brick on the table. It seemed crazy but it was like a dream come true. When other kids wanted to be doctors and lawyers, Ali wanted to be a big-time drug dealer. That all he knew and all he saw when he was younger. It was no looking back now, it was on and popping. He meticously cut the wrapper off the brick. It was wrapped in duct tape, rubber inner tube and truck grease. After getting it all the way out of the wrapper he was greeted by a smell that was like no other. The kilo itself had the Chanel double c stamped in the middle of it and it was so shiny and pretty that he didn't want to even break it. He felt good because he went from a Nick to a Brick!!!!

Later that night in the Pub, Ali was on fire. He popped a spider man x pill and was showing out. He was buying everybody drinks he knew. He saw C-Lo and told him that he wanted to holla at him. They were still tight but they were doing their own separate thing. "Dawg, I brought my first brick today" Ali said happy for himself but when he told C-Lo he could feel the vibe that C-Lo wasn't on that level. He caught that and told C-Lo to come and fuck with him and he didn't have to spend no money.

Aaron street was back wide open so that's where the crew was hanging at. Ali was copping a brick at least once a week. He had Pretty cooking all his crack for him and buying work as well from him. He sat back and saw that it was really booming at the trap. He knew right then that it was money to be made in Orangeburg.

Ali was thinking that he was going to buy Rashawn her first car. It wasn't her birthday or anything but he had so much money coming in that he had money to blow. He went to the Mitsubishi lot in Columbia and brought a 2002 Mitsubishi Galant cash for his girl. When he pulled up to the apartment he jumped out and ran inside and told Rashawn to come outside and when she saw the car she asked who car was it. He handed her the keys and said it was hers. Tears started to roll down her. Ali was treating real damn good. At times, she felt as if she didn't deserve that and regretted ever cheating on him.

"You going to suck it for me" Ali asked Monee. Monee was a bad red bone from St. Matthews that Ali was fucking. Ali remembered Monee was one of the baddest bitches at Calhoun County High School. He always said that he wanted her and now he had her.

"You going to eat my pussy?"

"I don't eat no pussy"

"Well I don't suck no dick". They had already fucked twice but Ali loved to see that red ass bounce up and down on his dick. Ali phone started to ring. He had been missing in action for about 3 hours fucking with Monee. To make it bad he was creeping in Rashawn's car. He didn't recognize the number so he ignored it. Then when he was about to stick his dick in Monee juice box his phone ranged again. This time when he looked at it Jet number was on the caller id. "What they do" Ali asks when he answers

"Guess who just called me"

"Who"

"My cousin O-Zone"

"Oh yeah"

"Guess what"

"What"

"He out and over there on the block". That was all that needed to be said. He asked what number did he call from and Jet recited the number and that was the same number that had called him a few minutes earlier. Jet was saying some slick shit on the low but Ali wasn't trying to hear it. "Let me call you back in a minute, I'm with my baby Monee right now and we about to get it in real quick". Ali was trying to get off the phone so he could call and see what O-Zone had going on.

Ali called the number back and smiled when he heard O' Zone voice. "What kind of bird don't fly" Ali asks

"A jail bird but this bird done flew the coop" O-Zone laughs

"Where you at"

"At the spot on State Court"

"I'll be there in a second". Ali gave Monee a kiss and left.

When Ali pulled up to the spot he saw that the porch light was off but he could see a shadow on the porch.

"What's up my nigga" Ali asks

"I done beat them crackers again" O-Zone went on to give Ali the run down on how he beat the feds again! He was pulling out all kind of paperwork to show Ali but Ali was like 'fuck all that, what you going to do'.

"What you mean"

"I'm out here, you know where it is just point me in the right direction" Ali asked O-Zone couldn't believe it but had to smile at the hungriness in Ali. Here it was O-Zone came back from the point of no return. Nobody beats the feds and he did it twice and wants to throw the towel in but Ali wants to go hard in the paint.

"I'm trying to get married and move to Miami and just lay it down" he said but Ali wasn't trying to hear that at all. Ali kicked it to O-Zone about how niggas been dragging him since he was gone and how niggas was talking shit about him. He also lets him know that he was trying to buy two if the price was right. Before the conversation was over Ali was getting pointed in the right direction. At the numbers that he was getting quoted he told his big homie that he would hit him off each one of them.

Ali wanted to put his truck in the shop to shut shit down. He hooked up with Big Snake from Hwy 4. Big Snake was another heavy hitter from the Burg. He was from out the country part but was getting real paper. Ali started fucking with him when he was going to the Pub. He use to get money off the white girl but he left that alone and went with the Tiger Woods (Weed). He was telling Snake one night that he wanted to do his truck up and Snake knew just the place if he wanted to spend some money. Ali didn't want to go half ass, he wanted to go all out. They ended up in Moneta, SC at Salter's paint and body. That white boy there could paint his ass off. He even had a few cars of his featured in the low rider magazines, he knew his shit. 2 hrs later and 20 stacks changing hands, the Expo was left to get tricked out.

Ali was getting ready to bring his 23rd b-day in with a bang. He had got in contact with the boys who was renting out the Club Static (formerly the Ritz) to rent the whole club out for his B-Day. They just couldn't understand what Ali was trying to do because Ali said everything was free. Free drinks, free admission and free food. "I have never been to a birthday party when I was little and had to pay for anything" Ali told them.

Chapter 16
'I Put On For My City'

Ali sat in his apartment with his sentry safe open counting stacks, "97,98,99,100" he counted out loud. He couldn't believe his eyes, he had 100 stacks in the stash not counting his re-up money! Stash money. He hasn't been out a whole 2 years yet and he was on top of his game. He called Rashawn in the room and told her to go look for a house because he had too much money to be staying in the apartment.

Ali pulled up to the club and pop the doors on the truck and let the doors go up. It was like a paparazzi was out there. Cameras and camera phones was going off snapping pictures. The Expo was the first in South Carolina with the lambo doors. He had the truck tricked all the way out and everybody was loving it.Ali did it big for his bday. He planned to shut the city down and that he did. It was the talk of town for weeks about the free everything and they came to see if it was real. He put on for his city

About a week after his 23rd bday party Ali had to put his pistol game down. One night while at Club Dazzlers Ali was partying hard. He was on X and grey goose and getting loose. He was by the bathroom trying to get with this girl named Tina. Tina was thicker than mustard and had a sexy gap between her teeth and legs. While he was trying to put his bid in and get the digits his phone rings. He looks and see that it's his brother Sidney so he answers and when he does he thinks that he hear his brother say that he got robbed or some shit like that. He told Tina that he would get at her later and went outside so that he could hear better. "What you say"

"Lil Bro come up to the house, some shit went down" Sidney says. It was nothing else to be said. They may not talk for weeks at a time but they both had each other back, they were just like that, they held each other down. He sped up to Sidney trailer on Rainfall rd. and when he got there Sidney was standing there in the yard in all black.

"What's the deal" Ali asks

"Somebody just tried to kick my door in" he said

"You alright"

"Yeah, I'm good but they tried to kicked the door off the hinges" Sidney says as he shows Ali the damage that was done. He was telling Ali what all that happen and when he finally got to the door he saw a gray Honda pulling off. They couldn't figure out who drove the Honda but they were going to find out and make somebody pay for the violation.

A few days later Ali got the news he wanted. He got out of his car and approached Sidney. "I know who tried to pull that jack move on you"

"Who"

"It's that jack boy Brad from New York, Vinny and that pussy King boy that I shot a few years back." He got the news from some niggas that be getting high with them. Brad had been down south for a while pulling jack moves. He has a few bodies under his belt but he usually tricks a nigga to do the dirty work. 'And that's not the good part"

"What's up"

"I got Vinny right where I want him, I'm serving him"

"What the fuck wrong with you, you know how them niggas get down"

"I know, that's how I'm going to bait his ass and put that fuck nigga to sleep". They both knew how Brad gets down. That was he would buy dope from a nigga a few times to see what he is working with and then turn around and rob the nigga. "I served him yesterday off the brick so that he could see that I got it". They talked for an hour on how they were going to give the jack boys a permanent dirt nap.

The next Saturday night Ali called Sidney bumping that Lil Wayne "Lights Out". "Yo, big bro, go to the met and get you something to drink and have a good time". Sidney didn't have to question why Ali said to go have a drink when Ali knew Sidney never smoked or dranked a day in his life. Ali was telling him to have an alibi

CHAPTER 17
WHAT HAPPEN TO THAT BOY

"Yeah, meet me in Roosevelt Gardens" Ali said thru the phone

"Alright son, I will be there in about 20 minutes." Vinny told Ali before they disconnected. Ali didn't think that it was strange that Vinny wanted to get a quarter bird when he was used to getting an ounce. Ali also didn't think twice that it was dark and late night either. Ali knew what the lick was and that Vinny was trying to rob him.

Ali was sitting back in his car in the circle of Roosevelt Gardens playing C-Murder's "Down for my niggas", when Vinny pulled up in the same gray Honda that Sidney described leaving his house. Vinny was a dead man walking for sure. He was already going to die for the violation but now he had to die that night. Ali let his window down and told Vinny that it was to out in the open and that he wanted to go over by Brookdale Middle school and to follow behind him.

Ali pulled out of the gardens and headed to Shadow Lawn rd. with his victim following him. Ali pulled on behind the school house and hopped out of his vehicle and approached Vinny's Honda on the passenger side. He thought that Vinny's was going to wind the window down but he unlatched the door so Ali jumped in. "Hey playboy, you wanted a 9 piece right"

"Yeah that's what I want" Vinny said. Ali reached in his hoody pocket but instead of pulling out a 9 piece of cocaine he pulled out a 9mm Smith and Wesson. It was already cocked and off safety so Ali fired and shot Vinny in the right side of the chest. Vinny screamed and his eyes grew large with terror. He was trying to figure out what went wrong but while doing so Ali was asking questions like why did he try to rob his brother. Vinny started pleading saying he didn't know what he was talking about. Ali got madder and shot him again, "Bitch don't play with me, you know what I'm talking about."

"Who you talking about?"

"Sidney nigga" and Ali shot him again. Vinny could feel his life slipping away and inside the car was getting too hot for him so he was trying to exit the car and Ali shot him once again. Vinny managed to get out the car and stumbled to the ground. Ali jumped out the passenger side and ran around to the driver's side where Vinny was trying to get to his feet.

"Bitch nigga look at me before I kill you" Ali said to him. When Vinny looked up at Ali he knew it was over with. One shot to the head and he was out of here. Not one to miss and opportunity, Ali searched Vinny to see if he had the money or anything on him and all he found was a Hi-Point 380. Ali thought 'Broke big foot mutha fucker'. He searched the car and wiped it down before heading to his car and got in and took off.

On the way back home he called Sidney and when he answered the phone Ali said "What happened to that boy" mimicking Baby from the song he was playing. They both laughed and disconnected the phone.

That Sunday just as always when Ali pushes a nigga to the other side he went to church to repent and ask for forgiveness. He doesn't feel anyway about it because he never gives a nigga the business who doesn't deserve it. While in the small church in St. Matthews he reflects on his life and decides that he wants to go to college and further his education.

The next day Ali enrolled in Denmark Technical college and majored in Computer Technology. He sees it as a challenge and something good that will benefit him.

CHAPTER 18
DEATH COMES IN 3'S

"What the fuck is this" Ali asks Stink

"that's the 2 bricks you ordered"

"Why it looks like this". Ali asked and Stink shrugs his shoulders and was like that's how it came. The way it was set up was when Ali gets to the "A", he gives the money to Stink who counts the money and then goes somewhere else to get the work. Up until this point everything has been going smoothly and it has been well over 10 trips. He is just looking at the work which is not in its normal packaging but in a freezer bag. He grabs one of the bricks and it crumbles and all Ali can think about is the T.I. song when he said 'it's that touch and bust shawty'. He really feels that is some shit in the game and that the niggas were trying to play him. They go back and forth for about an hour on what was wrong. Stank was trying to get him to open one of the keys up and check the work but Ali is no fool and know the rules to the game. You open it up, it's yours!

Ali is now trying to get Stank to take the dope back and get some more or get his money back. But now all of a sudden Stink cannot get in contact with who he got the dope form. Ali had gotten comfortable with them so he wasn't even strapped. It was getting late so he decided to leave and go home but told Stink that he was leaving the dope but he was coming back in the morning and to have his money. Ali had already blanked out and had murder on his mind.

Once back in Orangeburg Ali goes to one of his partner Nook trailer in Dog Wood trailer park. His nigga kept plenty of straps. "Dawg I need some fire power"

"What you need"

"Something to knock a nigga head off with"

"What the drama be about"

"Niggas got me fucked up, playing with my money" Ali said and then went on to tell Nook what went down. Nook was ready to ride but Ali wasn't with that. He didn't know how Nook would hold up under pressure because he knew he was about to act a damn fool. "Naw I got this, if I don't make it back you know what it is." O-Zone had been hitting Ali's phone all night but Ali pressure was up and his head was hurting and already made up. He didn't need nobody trying to talk sense or be diplomatic about the situation.

Ali couldn't sleep at all that night so the next morning he jumped in Rashawn's car and went to this chick Carmen's house to ask her to drive for him. She had been trying to fuck with him and screaming that she was down for whatever, so he was about to give her something to do. "I need you to drive me to the 'A' to pick up some money"

"Alright, when you want to go"

"Now". That's was all that needed to be said.

On I-20, Ali had Trick Daddy's "Bout my money" on repeat. Carmen was on the phone talking to one of her girlfriends. That was all the better for Ali because he didn't feel like talking and wanted to stay focused. He wasn't answering the phone for nobody and he saw that O-Zone called a few times....

Unbeknownst to Ali, earlier that morning O-Zone and Stink put a plan together and had the two kilos of cocaine shipped to Orangeburg via UPS. They put the work in a gutted-out computer and next day aired it.

After Carmen and Ali got off on the Flat Shoals exit, he got her to pull to a gas station that was about a 5-minute walk to Stink's trap. He pulled out a wad of money and gave Carmen $500 and told her to go get some gas and to go to the lil strip plaza and go in a few stores and shop or whatever and then jumped out the car and went on his mission.

Knock knock knock. "Who dat"? "Me, who you think". After looking thru the blinds on the window Stink lets Ali in. "Damn shawty, I aint know you been coming"

"I told you I was coming back in the morning"

"You ain't talk to O-Zone"

"Naw, for what"

"Because we mailed it to you this morning" Stank said but Ali looked at him like 'you really think that I'm a slow ass country nigga. After listening to the story about the dope was on the way and how he was supposed to get it, Ali was even more upset now because he was told that it was the same dope that he didn't want the day before. He pulled his strap from his fatigue pants and pointed directly at Stinks head. "What's happening shawty" was all he could get out of his mouth before he was slapped upside the head with the pistol. "Get that fuck nigga on the phone" Ali said to him

"O-Zone said that he would call me back because he had something to do"

Ali slaps him upside the head again and lets him know he was not talking about O but was talking about the nigga that sold him the bullshit ass dope. Stink was talking some bullshit but after about 10 slaps with the pistol he was convinced that it was best to make the call to where he got the dope from.

A fat dude pulled up the spot and jumped out of a late model Chevy pickup truck. He had on a blue dickie suit with a name tag and logo of his detail shop. Without knocking he walked into the trap and into hell. "Get the fuck over there" Ali tells him with the pistol pointed in his face. Sam looks at Ali and see that he has a lot on his mind and then looks at Stink who is a bloody mess and decides to listen to the orders that he is given. "Where the fuck my money at" Ali questions him. Sam then goes to acting stupid like he didn't know what Ali was talking about. This enrages Ali, so he starts to pistol whip Sam also. Sam was really on some other shit saying "Dope man paid, money gone". After that Ali decided to take it as a loss and shot Sam and Stink in the chest. When the both rolled off the couch they were on he placed a bullet in both of their heads. 'I'll do life about mine.

Ali left the house as quiet as he came. On the way back he called Carmen to see where she was at and found out that she was getting her nails done and was just about finished. When he reached to where she was he let her know that he was ready to get back on the road. After stopping and getting some grey goose they hit I-20. Within 10 minutes Ali smashed the whole 5th of goose.

CHAPTER 18
PENTENTIARY CHANCES

Ali feel asleep after drinking the goose and listening to Lil Wayne's Carter 1 cd. When he woke up he could not have been in the worst situation. Carmen was pulling over and blue lights was on behind them. "What the fuck going on" he asks her and she responds that she think that she was speeding. All he could think about was going to jail, he still had the murder weapon on him.

The cop came to the window and let Carmen know that she was doing 89 in a 70. All he could think of how the fuck did he let that happen. And if things couldn't have gotten worst, when the officer asked Carmen for her license and registration she started stuttering so bad that it sounded like she was talking in tongues. The officer asks her to get out the car and they walked back to the patrol car. Ali took the pistol off him and locked it in the glove compartment. After about 5 minutes she came back to the car and Ali asked her what happened and she said that he wanted to search the car.

"So, what did you tell him" he asks with not wanting to know.

"I told him yeah, you don't have anything in here do you"

"I don't have nothing but the pistol". By this time, it was about 10 police cruisers with lights on behind their car. They both were asked to step out of the car and then separated. They were questioned and asked over and over about where the drugs and money was located at in the car.

The drug K-9 dog never alerted on the car after being taken around the car several times. The black officer even went so far as to open all the doors and put the dog inside the car to see if that position would help the dog smell better. After all of this, the other officers laughed at the 1st officer for making a fool of himself. Even against police protocol the officer searched the vehicle. When he reached the glove compartment he acted as if he found a jack pot. The officer then ran the gun but it came back clean. Ali just knew that his life was over with being caught with a gun that had two fresh bodies on it. His mind started playing tricks on him because he was thinking that the officer could feel the heat coming off the gun. Even thou the gun came back clean he still locked Ali up for being in possession of a gun as a convicted felon.

McDuffie County jail

"Yo yo" O-Zone answers the phone

"What's up my nigga" Ali responds

"I been trying to call you but you never picked up"

"I fucked up big homie, I just got jammed on the 'I' with a pistol"

"Pistol, what they fuck you doing with a gun" O-Zone said thinking about how wild these young boys are

"I don't even know, I just lost it" Ali said and left it at that. After a minute of silence, he told O-Zone what he was charged with and O-Zone let him know what the outcome could be if it goes federal. Ali just wanted to get a bond so he could get out and fight the case from the outside. O-Zone let him know if he got a bond he would come get him the same day.

"I have been trying to call Stink back after he mailed the pair of shoes that you came to get yesterday"

"Oh yeah" was all that Ali could say

"That nigga probably sleeping"

"Yeah, he maybe just resting" Ali said and thinking resting in peace (R.I.P.) with an evil grin.

The next morning Ali found out that he was sleeping for about an hour before they got pulled over. Being that far away from the crime scene helped a lot because they were none the wiser that they had the murder weapon used in a double homicide. He was given a 5-thousand-dollar cash bond and he was out in no time. Carmen and Pretty was there when he got out and all he could scream "What yall thought yall wasn't going to see me". Carmen lets him know that O-Zone will be in town later that night and wanted to see him. Ali jumped in the back seat and went into a zone thinking about if his homie knew that Stink and his brother in law was dead and if he did how he felt about it. He wanted to know how their relationship stood after the stunt that he pulled, but before any of that he wanted to know about the 2 kilos that was supposed to be mailed to him. He just hoped that the murders didn't come up with the gun. He now really needed the dope so that he could get his money up to fight his case.

"What they do" Ali answers his cell

"I'm outside" was all that O-Zone said and disconnected. Ali got up and threw on a tank top and some black Sean Jean jeans and all black tims. He grabbed is 38 blue steel revolver and slipped it in his back pocket just in case he needed.

"What's up homie" Ali said after getting into the car.

"What the fuck wrong with you" O-Zone asked pissed at Ali for what he had done.

"What you talking about" Ali said playing stupid

"You killing all these niggas around here like this a 3rd world country and shit, look here man, I know it's you that putting in work around here but you can't get money and bust your gun. It isn't gonna work! I hear that your name is coming up in the murder over there by the middle school too." O Zone was saying while looking at Ali to see if he was soaking it all in or just saying fuck it.

"When bodies start coming up dead, that brings too much heat. They will let you sell dope all day but they not about to let their murder rate increase." He put it all out there. Ali just sat there like a child being admonished by a parent. "You can't keep taking these penitentiary chances" Ali just shook his head as if he understood.

CHAPTER 19

'DIFFERENT CLASS RIGHT HERE'

"Who dis" Ali said after answering his cell phone.

"Tiffany" the unknown female caller said

"Tiffany who"

"The girl you gave your number to in the club". For the past few weeks Ali been playing the phone game with this female on his phone. He never gives his number out without knowing who the person is. She had a nice voice too, so Ali played along with the female sometimes.

"What you doing this weekend?"

"Me and my baby moms going to Mexico"

"Must be nice"

"Just taking a little vacation to get away from the Burg"

"I wish I could go to Mexico" she said. Ali had to take the opportunity to get a little stunt on. "Who is your man? If you were my woman this the shit that I like to do". This was his first time traveling out the country but he knew that it would not be his last. After getting caught with that pistol and not knowing the outcome to that situation, he decided it was time to have fun and enjoy his money. 'beep' Ali phone lets him know that he has a call coming in and it was O-Zone. With Ali, it's always M.O.B. Money over bitches and Money over Bullshit. "Girl from the club that I just met and gave my number too but I don't remember, could you call me back in about an hour". She agreed and hung up.

"What they do"

"Where you at"

"Where you need me to be"

"Come to the spot-on State Court"

"Be there in 10"

Ali pulled up to the spot and got out to holla at O-Zone. "What you know good" he asked

"One of my peoples got murdered up in the 'A' and I'm up here for the funeral." O-Zone responded

"Who got killed"

"Hack".

"Damn" was all Ali could say. Hack was another one of 0-Zone plugs. He was in good with some niggas in the 'A' and had work out the ass. Hack and O-Zone went to school together and played ball. Ali had gotten more than enough keys from Hack. Now with him killing Stink and Sam and Hack coming up dead, he seemed to be losing all his connects. "So, what you going to do, you don't know nobody else?" he asked

"I still got some folks down bottom, I'm going to holla at them when I get back to see what's up"

"Do that, you know that I'm on deck."

MIAMI FL.

Ali and Rashawn was about to board the Carnival Cruise ship destined for Cozumel, Mexico. He stood back and watched the beautiful scene before him and loved what he saw. I could get use to this is what he was thinking. His cell phone rings and he picks it up and see that it is Nick. They kicked it for a few minutes and then Ali let Nick know that he would be gone for 5 days but he wanted to see him when he gets back.

"I know you needed to see me, I was waiting on you to call me, you getting front door service and you want to drive 3 hrs and get jammed on the road" Nick says

"How the hell you know that"

"I know who you been fucking with when you cut me off, I just want to know why"

"You know how it is, niggas had cheaper numbers"

"Well them niggas dead now, so I know that you would call sooner or later" Nick said. Ali was wondering how he knew so much and would he fuck with him still. He told Ali to hit him up when he gets back so they could discuss some numbers. With that Ali was ready to blow some money because he knew he would get it right back.

Cozumel, Mexico

"Hey babes" Ali says while shaking Rashawn trying to wake her up. They just reached Mexico and he wanted to go ahead and go sightseeing. After getting her up he went to the top deck to see what he could see. Once he got there he saw this chick that he had been seeing since he got on the ship. She was at the ice cream machine getting a sundae made. Ali looked at her and something about her was making him very intrigued. She was about 5ft4, 130 pounds with a nice ass and breasts with a short haircut like the singer Monica but she was just jazzy as hell. She had on a pair of coach sneakers with the bag to match. Ali decided that would be his approach to her.

"Excuse me, where did you get that Coach bag from" Ali asked after he got her attention.

"The Coach store" she said with much attitude. That turned Ali off and he turned around to walk away before he said something even slicker to her. But before he could walk away she said "Why? You don't know nothing about or buy Coach"

"Why you say that"

"Because I see you and your girl and yall are all urban, with the Sean Jean, Baby Phat and Roca Wear"

"What's wrong with that?"

"Oh nothing, this just a different class right here".

Ali was getting pissed with how this bitch was talking all out the way. "What the fuck that supposed to mean?"

"Don't get offended boo, but if you want a hood chick or project chick, that's what you buy but if you want a bank manager, lawyer or professional woman like myself then this is what you buy" After that Ali and the chick had about a 30-minute conversation. He found out that her name was Sherina and she graduated from SCSU. She was now working as a bank manager in the Cayman Island.

"There go Miss. Baby Phat right there" she says and nods towards the door. Rashawn just stepping in and was Baby Phat from head to toe. Ali just smiled and shook his head and thought to himself 'fuck what she talking about, my baby still looks good. He met her and they went to the buffet and had a quick breakfast and headed to exit the boat.

"Damn, its hot and muggy out here" Ali said while waiting on a rental car. It was very hot and muggy but he was going to enjoy being out of the country. They got the car and started cruising the island. They went into a few shops and stores but it was nothing to buy as far as clothes but Rashawn did see a tattoo shop that she wanted to go in and get a tat.

While Rashawn was getting a tattoo, Ali wandered around to find some Amigos to see if they had some weed. About 5 minutes later, Ali was behind the shop smoking some Bobby Brown (dirt weed). It wasn't the best but the way they had the blunt stuffed with weed, he was high as hell mid-way thru.

Being high and in a zone had Ali thinking about how life been treating him lately. He was straight. 100 grand in the stash, 3 cars and here he was in another country smoking weed and just enjoying himself. "I love this life right here".

CHAPTER 20
NOTHING BEATS THE CROSS BUT THE DOUBLE CROSS!

October 2004

"I usually don't mix business with pleasure, but I'm going to fuck with you" Ali told Sherina. Before he left Mexico, he ended up switching numbers with her and they had been fucking around ever since. This was the third time she came over to visit him and the second time they had sex. Fucking with her seemed to have all kind of benefits and perks. She had been telling him about some of her cousins that she had on the island and how he was caked up with work for the low. 15 grand a key was damn good and Ali couldn't pass that up. The deal was he give her 60 grand and she get the work from her cousin and then he takes a cruise over there and take the work back. He gave her the money without a second thought. Under normal circumstances a dope boy would not take a risk or gamble like that. But since he was fucking her and felt close to her, he decided to risk it. Well that and the fact she introduced him to her mother and took in to her house in Dillion SC. Her mother's life was not worth 60 grand he figured?

3 weeks later, Cayman Island

After getting off the cruise ship, Ali and Rashawn went on a shopping spree. In less than 2 hours they spent over $5000. He kept looking at his watch because he knew that he had to go to the bank and meet Sherina and get the work. While they were shopping, they spotted another tattoo shop and

Rashawn wanted another one. That was good for Ali because he had to get away for a few.

Ali walked in the bank and walked straight to where Sherina said her office was located at. Ali stood in the office door way and when she looked up he said "What you thought you wasn't going to see me?". After telling her coworkers she was going on break, they left and got into her small Nissan Sentra. It was Ali turn to give her a hard time "Damn, I aint never seen a professional woman in a car this small" and started laughing. She punched him in the arm and told him not to be talking about her baby. She took him to her house and told him to get the bag out the coat closet.

Inside the closet in a grey Prada bag was 4 perfectly wrapped kilos. With the sight of that, Ali dick gets brick hard. He didn't know if he wanted to fuck Sherina who was looking sexy as hell in her business suit of did he want to fuck the 4 white bitches (kilos) looking at him. Ali gave her 4 stacks for getting the work for him. She was also telling him about how good it was for him to put money in the bank over there just in case shit got funky in the States, so he gave her another 5 stacks to open a bank account at the bank. He just figured that it would be a good thing to do.

Nov. 2004

"What's up Tip" Ali said

"What you called me" the female caller said

"I said what's up Tip, that's your name right"

"Oh yeah, I just didn't hear you"

"So, when I'm going to get to see you mystery girl"

"Why you want to see me?"

"Because you be using all my daytime minutes and I want to see who I'm spending my money on"

"Can you meet me tonight?"

"Just give me the time and place and I will be there"

"Meet me @ Fatz @ 9 in the parking lot in the back"

"Bet, I'll be there"

At 9 on the dot, Ali was pulling up in his silver 2002 Monte Carlo he just bought playing Project Pat "Mister don't play" cd. He pulled in the parking lot in the back sitting low behind dark tint. He dialed Tip number and she picked up on the first ring. "What car you in" he asked. "the tan Honda" she responded. When he saw which car it was he pulled up and parked beside it. Once he noticed who was driving the Honda he was shocked to say the least, because it was Aaron's baby mother Isis. He could only think "Nothing beats the cross but the double cross!!"

One week later Ali was leaving Club Dazzlers and was headed to Isis house off the Bellville rd. He pulled up and she came outside and got into the Expo. They started talking and he told Isis that he was tired and needed to get some sleep and she told him that she wanted to ride around for a minute.

"If we leave here, I'm not bringing you back" he let Isis know

"Ok let's go" was all that needed to be said.

They pulled into the Fairfield Inn off 601 and got a suite. When they made it to their room he gave her one of his rules. "I like to sleep naked and whoever gets in the bed with me got to be naked also." Without having to say nothing else, Isis came out of her clothes. Her butterscotch complexion made her body so enticing that Ali get instantly hard. After getting into bed they began to kiss and feel and rub each other. After about 5 minutes Ali couldn't take it anymore. He had to see how good the pussy was, he rolled over and got between her legs and was about to penetrate but stopped so he could see how the inside of her pussy looked. He saw the prettiest pinkest pussy he ever laid eyes on. It didn't look like a baby came out of there let alone two kids. No stretch marks anywhere, so he knew he was about to enjoy himself. He grabbed his dick and put the tip of his head in her pussy and she started sliding back. He could feel the tightness of her love box "I told you that I was celibate, since I my baby father went to jail so take it slow." He then started going easy with his thrust until he got it all the way in. The whole time she was making sexy fuck faces and moaning that was turning Ali on to the 100th power. They fucked about an hour straight, she had about 2 orgasms and was trying to get a 3rd. Ali felt himself about to come so he told her that he was about to bust, and she said she was about to also. He came a few seconds later and shot it all inside of her.

CHAPTER 21
DOING BIG BOY THINGS

Ali, Jet, Nook and Gemini was in Miami to go to the Source Awards. They were hitting up the mall and flea markets hard. After doing their shopping they went to their hotel on South Beach.

Ali and O-Zone told the rest of the boys that they were going to go back to the mall and grab something. The real reason for them leaving was for 0-Zone to introduce Ali to one of his Cuban plugs. The Cubans had a booth at the flea market that sold everything to do with drugs. They had cut, scales, bags, safes compressors and whatever else you needed. The introduction and the conversation went well. It went so good that Ali told them that he could move 5 keys a week if he had access to it. They agreed to a price of 100 grand for 5 keys. The Cubans was feeling the savvy Ali so much that they gave him 5 keys then and told Ali that he would send somebody down the next week to pick up the money and bring 5 more. The only thing Ali could think of was Orangeburg was about to be in trouble.

At the Source Awards the boys got to act up. The was drinking and having a good ol' time. Lil Wayne, Trick Daddy, and David Banner performed as well as countless others. All Ali could think about was all the money he was about to make. He was doing the math in his head. He could sell each Big 8 for 3 stacks a piece and come out with 24 grand each brick, with 5 bricks he could make at least 20 thousand profit on each flip. He knew that he could work with that.

After getting back from Miami, Ali went to his secret apartment on Shadow Lawn to see what the work was like that he got from the Cubans. He trafficked the 5 keys back in the Ford Excursion that they rented. They were even pulled over but the truck was not searched. That had him feeling untouchable. When he got there, he opens and checked all the keys. Then he took out a quarter brick and headed to Pretty's house to see what it could do in the water. Pretty put his whip game down, he made the dope do numbers. Ali knew it was on, he now had some good hard white in the city.

Ali was on the phone kicking it with Isis while he counted all the money he made that day. "Ali, did you go all the way the other night" she asked him.

"What you mean"

"Hmmm, did you pull out"

"Naw, I don't think that I did" he said knowing damn well he busted inside of her. They talked a little more and she was telling him that she was feeling the same way she felt on the last two pregnancies.

December 2004

DJ Dirty put together a ballers vacation for some niggas that was making money in the city. He was a dj that was down with rapper Grand Daddy Souf and Three 6 Mafia. Grand Daddy Souf was down with the new middle weight champion Antonio Tarver. So it was set for the ballers of the city to fly out to L.A. for the Antonio Tarver and Glenn Johnson fight at the Staples Center.

Ali, DJ Dirty, O-Zone, Pretty, Twin and Gizmo landed at the L.A.X. and picked up two rental Tahoe trucks and headed to the W hotel.

"Damn, that dude beating Tarver ass out there" Ali says to DJ Dirty. He responded by saying that's how Tarver fights and he going to get back. Well Tarver must have waited too late because Glen Johnson whipped Tarver ass that night. After the fight as they left out of the Staple Center leaving the fight, they spotted some bitches that were jocking them since they got to the fight so they went over to fuck with them. After they politic for a few they exchanged numbers and said they would get up the next day.

The next day Ali and the crew pulled up on Crenshaw Blvd and went to the bitches' house that the met the night before. It was like a mini after party, everybody was having a good time. The chick that he was fucking with put in another cd. Boyz N Da Hood song "Dem Boyz" started bumping from the system and everybody was feeling the music. Ali asked the chick who that was and she replied that it was Big Meech's group.

"Who is Big Meech".

"That's the nigga that run B.M.F." She said That was about the third or fourth time that he heard of BMF, the first time was when 'Hack' said that he was dealing with them, so he asked the chicks what was that. They went to telling stories of how the down south boys come over there and put on and made plenty of noise. They alone made it to where they respected niggas from the East Coast.

Jan 05

T.I. song "Let's get away" plays as Ali ringtone for Isis. "What's up babes" Ali answers. "Nothing much, we getting up tonight?" "It's whatever you want to do" he lets her know. Ever since he layed the dick game down on her, they were fucking like every day. Their favorite spot was the Fairfield Inn.

About 2 rounds of sex, Ali told Isis that he was going to this new club called Nu Vibe in Summerton SC. He was tired of staying in the city and partying with the local jokers all the time. He had money and his money was real long, long enough to shine wherever he went. "When you come back you going to put your thing on my butt?" Isis asked with a devilish smile. She loved to sleep naked and for Ali to hold her all night so she could feel his dick on her ass all night. "You know I got you" He said and then took a shower and headed to the club.

Club Nu Vibe

Ali walked in the club with a lot of the homies from the city. He was feeling himself because he felt like no nigga could touch him with the dope game. His hustle game was up to the top and still going. He went to the bar and started fucking with the bartender with the fat ass and big nose, he ordered bottles of Grey Goose, Patron and Moet. He popped the bottle of Moet and took a triple stack Tracey MacGrady X-pill and was starting to feel real lovely in the spot. He was at the bar doing what he does best, that's get fucked up and fuck with the bartenders. He looked over and saw his lil mans DT being very disrespectful trying to pull every bitch he saw. He was telling them hoes to "drop that zero and get with a hero" and all other kind of shit. All Ali could do was shake his head and laugh at how he was showing out. Ali went back to trying to get the bartender number when a fight broke out. It didn't take long for him to figure out that DT had gotten into some shit. He grabbed his Moet bottle off the bar and went into the melee, when he spotted his lil mans on the bottom of the pile he swung the bottle and tried to knock a nigga brains out with the bottle. CRACK! The bottle sounded as it met with a skull. The nigga dropped but Ali was surprised that the bottle didn't break. "Fuck it" he thought and swung again, the second time it struck another skull and another victim fell. He misjudged the next swing and lost his grip on the bottle. With no weapon, Ali had to result to using his hand skills and it was an all-out brawl after that. Before security broke the fight up, Ali had about 3 niggas on top of him getting off. As security was escorting him out the club he had one thing on his mind, MURDER. When he reached his truck he realized that he was not strapped. Then like an answer to his prayers he saw this kid named Fred from Roseville walking to his car with a busted lip. "My nigga you strapped" he asked Fred and as he popped the trunk and pulled out a Glock 40. Pac and DT was shaking their head no to indicate to Fred not to give Ali the tool. "I'm about to kill one of them niggas" Ali said. Fred thought about how his mouth was bleeding and was like fuck it and gave him the gun.

Ali sprinted back to the front door of the club wanting to see any of the niggas he got into it with. When he spotted the dark skin dude with the dreads, he pulled the glock out and ran up on the nigga "What's up now nigga" was all he said and when dread head realized that he was in trouble and that Ali had the draw on him, he was already getting pumped full of lead. Ali emptied the clip and took off back toward the parking lot to where Fred was at and gave him the smoking gun. Fred was in shock and was thinking that this nigga is really crazy, 'he came and got my gun, went if front the club and dropped a nigga and give me my gun back like nothing happened at all'

CHAPTER 21
ALL BOSSES TAKE LOSSES

Feb 2005

"So, what happen to the money" Ali asks Rashawn. "I don't know" was all she kept saying. Ever since she gave birth to their little girl, Ali has been giving her money to put in a bank account for the daughter. He roughly calculated that it was over 20 grand that should be in the account. Now he had the bank statement that said it was less than 2 stacks in there. They argue for over an hour t the money until he decides that its best to leave before he does something that he will regret later. When it comes to his money, Ali would fuck anybody up, so he packs all his clothes and belongings and put them in his truck and Monte Carlo and tell Rashawn that he is leaving her. The only place he knows is the Fairfield Inn where he spends so much time with Isis, so that's where he gets a monthly rate to stay.

April 2005

"Isis what the fuck you doing" Ali asks her as she his searching the room up and down.

"Making sure that no other bitch been in here" she responded back. He thinks that she is crazy but love how fine she is at the same time. She is pretty much staying at the hotel with him and he can't complain about that. He decides to make her his main bitch and take it to another level. Fuck it, give the city something else to talk about.

He is doing pretty good for himself. He has a few different plugs so he always has work when his clientele needs it. 100 grand in the stash, a 6-figure nigga for real. He has one child and Isis is pregnant with another. It seems as if there is nothing but success on the horizon.

Just like that, as always, something pops off. Ali just got off the phone with one of his partners in the 'A' and he finds out that Nick got hit on the interstate with 2 kilos of cocaine.

May 2005

Ali and Sherina are onboard of the cruise ship headed on a 5-day trip to different islands. They are to first go to Nassau and Freeport Bahamas and then head to the Cayman Island. It's a vacation and a business trip all in one. He is massaging suntan lotion all over Sherina sexy body as they lay on the top deck of the ship. Ali squirts some lotion on his hands and puts them under her bikini bottoms and rubs the lotion onto her ass cheeks as she bites her bottom lip from the pleasure. Ali could tell that she is very excited because of the way she bites her lips and squeezing her eyes shut tight. He takes the opportunity to slip a finger in between her legs and instantly his finger becomes wet and warm. Sherina lets out a sexy moan and tell Ali that he needs to stop and they need to go back to their cabin. And to the cabin they went. And they fucked, made love and had sex the whole day at sea.

Cayman Island.

The next day Sherina and Ali made it to the bank where she worked so that she could get something out of her office. Ali waited outside to check the scenery out of the beautiful island and the people just walking about as if this was paradise. All he could think to himself was this was living life right here. Sherina came back out the bank with the keys to one of her coworkers car, "we going to drive Kim's car to go meet up with cuzo" she informs him. This was normal routine for Ali to pick the drugs up from one of many of her cousin's spots on the island. If he transported the kilo's back himself, he could save about 10 grand. He was getting a very sweet deal this time because he was getting 7 birds for 100 grand.

After about a 5-minute ride, Sherina turned on a street that they had been on before on several occasions to conduct business. While on the way over she told him that she tried to call her cousin and let him know that they were on the way but before she could finish telling him that, all her cousin said was come on and hung up. She said that her cousin sounded funny but thought nothing of it because her cousin stayed drunk or hung over from all the drinking that he did. Ali couldn't do nothing but laugh because her cousin and he got drunk a few times together and Ali didn't know who could out drink who. Once on the street Ali spotted 3 newer model sedans parked on the curb on the opposite side of the house they were going too. His senses and paranoia kicks in and he tells her not to stop and to keep going. As they pass the house, he looks but cannot tell if anything is out of place or out of the norm. After a good distant he instructs her to turn around and pull over on the side of the road. It's about a quarter mile down but Ali can see the spot from there. He tells her to text her cousin and tell him that they stopped to get something to eat and would be there in about an hour. After watching for about 20 minutes and not seeing anything out of the ordinary, he thinks that he is just being a little too paranoid. He tells her to go ahead and drive back to the spot. On the way back he spots a black guy in urban clothes come out a house across the street from the spot and walks toward one of the dark colored sedans he saw that spooked him earlier. He laughs to himself and thinks that he really is tripping because he thought it was the police. As their car gets closer, Ali watches the black guy pop the trunk to the car and reach in and pull out a jacket. When the black guy put the jacket on and turned around to get something else out the trunk, Ali heart dropped to his ass. The back of the jacket had big bold white letters DEA. Ali sits back low in the seat and tell Sherina not to stop and to keep going and she does so smoothly past the spot. He decides to go back closer to the ship. All he could think about was it was another setback and that it cost him $100 grand.

June 2005

Its Isis birthday and they are sitting in his room at the Fairfield Inn. She is 8 months now and showing really well, and he is rubbing her stomach and talking to his unborn child.

Ali has a lot on his mind, he thinks back to the losses that he has taken the last few months. How hard he must grind to get back as strong as he was. Then he knows that Isis baby father is about to get out of state prison and he has no way of knowing which way everything will play out. With them about to bring a child into this world, she let him know on numerous occasions that she is his now and that her past relationships or just that, the past. Ali believed and trusted her and decided to move forward with knowing he had her by his side.

After Ali took the lost in the Cayman Island, all he had was a little over a quarter kilo left and the money he had stashed in the bank account on the Island. He was back on the grind hard getting every dollar he could and stretching every gram that he had.

He knew that he had to reach out to his big homie for guidance on what he needed to do to get back ahead of the game and stay ahead. He let O-Zone know everything that happened and O-Zone let him know what the deal was "All Bosses, Take Losses"!!! 'it's just how you bounce back from it. Just like you got it one time before, you can get it again. Losing money is way better than losing your life or your freedom. While you are here you can make the money back, but if you are locked up you can't make no money'.

After soaking up the advice, he felt much better and told O-Zone that he was going to do it big again for his birthday at the end of the month and that he was invited and wasn't taking no for an answer. He missed the first one but was not going to miss this one.

While in the hospital with Isis and his baby boy, he is calling everybody to let them know about the little man coming into this world. He has plans to celebrate tonight and wanted everybody to come out and fuck with him. The whole time while he is at the hospital he keeps getting calls from an unknown number which he never answers. He decides to step out and take the call.

When he answered the phone, he knew exactly who it was when he heard the female voice. It was Asia, a thick redbone from Denmark that went to college with him. He smiled and thought about how much fun Asia and he had. He was thinking about how his dick use to get brick hard when she walked by him with those jersey dresses on and pretty feet hanging out. He was in another world thinking about how her body use to shake like she was having a seizure when she nutted until she brought him out of that wonderful daze and brought him back to earth when she said "I'm pregnant". It kept echoing in his ears. He was in shock to say the least. He knew that the condom broke several times while they were making love but he never stopped because the pussy was just so good. He knew that he planted that seed. He told Asia to call him later that night so they could discuss it more.

CHAPTER 22
"ALL EYES ON ME"

National Guard Armory

As the white stretch, Hummer pulled into the parking lot of the Armory, some of Orangeburg dope boy all-stars got amped at what lay ahead. Ali went all out again this year and rented out the National Guard Armory, went to Green's liquor store and spent over 5 grand on alcohol and got DJ Dirty to dj and had a caterer to do the food and it was all free again for the city. He got all the beautiful females that he knew to help bartend and work the doors.

Ali, C-lo, Pretty, T-Nasty, Shell Roc, Chopper, Dog and Ozone jumped out the Hummer and headed for the door. Before he could make it to the door Isis baby father stopped him and asked Ali "This is how you doing it" "I'm on a whole nother level now" Ali told Aaron and gave him a bottle of Grey Goose that he had the limo stocked with and told him to come inside and enjoy himself.

Once inside he forgot all about the drama in his life and felt good because of all the love he was getting from the crowd. The party was a big success again and it seemed as if everybody was having a good time. Jet's girlfriend Shakira came up to Ali and gave him a hug and wished him a happy birthday. As she gave him a hug she whispered in his ear "Be careful because I heard some of them Sprinkle boys over there hating and talking shit". All he could say was fuck them niggas and grabbed her hand and pulled it down to his side where his mini glock was and told her "I aint worried about nothing"

August 2005, Aaron St

Ali was posted up on Aaron St at Jet's spot. Jet had the spot back wide open and they were making plenty of noise on that side of town. The spot had plenty of drugs and that brought a pretty big crowd. Ali was trying to get his mind right so that he could start the fall semester at school. It was hard because he was making so much money and that made him focus more on his drug business then his school work. He also was concentrating on opening a car wash on Hwy 33 so that he could have a legit business going on. So just like that, it was time to celebrate. He sent some chicks that was over to the trap to the liquor store to get some drinks so they could get loose. Shakira pulled up and they talked for a few minutes. She was enrolled in school at South Carolina State and was getting ready to start school also. They exchanged numbers so that she could help him with his school work and to braid his hair because she said that she could do better than what it was looking like now.

October 2005
Homecoming

Ali was over to Shakira sister's apartment on Douglas McArthur getting his hair braided. That's where they would go whenever he got his hair and when she helped him with his school work. She got off the phone and asked could she party with him that night. She let him know that her boyfriend told her to ask him because he did not like to go out with her. He thought nothing of it and said sure.

That night Ali put on for the city again. He hit every club in the city to be seen and to spend some money. By the time they made it to the final club that night Shakira was beyond feeling good. After being in the club for about 30 minutes, Ali sat on the stage by the DJ and just sipped on a bottle of Moet. Shakira came over and sat in between his legs and rested her head on him. It was an innocent gesture but to the club it looked like much more. When he looked up he felt like 2Pac song "All eyes on Me".

A week later, Ali was on the phone with Shakira taking about an upcoming project due for his computer technology course. She was explaining the best way possible the he could handle the situation. Ali thought about the vibe that he was getting from her boyfriend for the past week. "Hey, what's up with your boyfriend" Ali asks.

"What you talking about"

"For the past week, he has not said over 3 words to me" Ali said. Shakira finally told him what the deal was. That night when they went to the club had everybody talking about they were fucking. A few niggas and bitches went back to tell Jet that something was going on, not only that, he believed what everybody was saying. Ali was thinking how crazy it was and how it confused him because Jet told her to ask him in the first place and his baby brother was with them. He wasn't tripping thou because that's how the city was. They would start rumors and make shit up. What got on his nerves and got him in his feelings was what else she told him. She let him know that Jet didn't want him over at the trap spot making money and thought that he was only making money because he was over there. That got him beyond pissed at that thought and was have always been about his money, he also made the comment that he wasn't his real homeboy anyway. He was glad that he knew Jet real feelings so now he could move forward. He tried but could not stop his slick mouth from talking. "Tell that nigga I get money, real money. I'm my own man and I don't have a boss man and I don't work for nobody! I got Sprint and Verizon, I don't need no trap I work off my phone". He hung up after that and thought how shit was when you started getting real money.

CHAPTER 23
FROM BREAK UPS TO MAKE UPS

January 06

Ali brought the new year in with the love of his life Isis. He couldn't be happier, he was getting plenty of money, had a bad bitch on his side, nothing else could be better. As he massaged her feet he knew that he had to come clean with his girl. "Isis, I have something to tell you and I hope that you don't hate me after this"

"What is it"

"I had another son in August" He just put it out there. Asia gave birth to his child and branded him with the letter A to start his name. Isis got so upset and angry that she kicked him in the face and went into the other room crying. He tried to explain but she wasn't trying to hear that, he was in the dog house for sure.

Feb 2006
Houston TX NBA All-Star Weekend

Once again DJ Dirty put a baller get away together. The music connects that he had was very beneficial. Dirty was good friends with Paul Wall and some other rappers in Houston TX. On this trip, DJ Dirty invited some niggas from Dirty Town. It was a kid named Ricky that was making money and plenty of noise in the city that Ali heard of from Bayne St that made the trip. Ali made a mental note to see what all Ricky knew and to see if they could do some business together in some kind of way. What he didn't know at the time was this trip would turn out to be a very good money making opportunity and the beginning of a very good friendship.

The Sharptown Mall was super pack with a crowd from all over the United States due to the fact that the All-Star game brought a great number of fans to whatever city it was held in. The trend now was that everybody was getting the diamond encrusted grills that rappers Mike Jones, Paul Wall and Slim Thug made famous. Ricky and Ali decided that they would be the first in Orangeburg to have the famous Paul Wall grill. While at the TV Johnny jewelry store Ali and Ricky kicked it, and talked about all kind of topics but Ali was more concerned about the drug game

As Ali was waiting to get fitted for his grill he ended up talking to a Mexican with a cowboy hat and cowboy boots on. The Mexican asked Ali did he fuck with weed, Ali in return told the Mexican he only fucked with cocoa leaves with a smile. That little exchanged led to a 20-minute conversation between the two that seemed to have plenty potential of becoming a beneficial friendship. The Mexican told Ali that he had some peoples on the east coast that he dealt with in Charlotte NC. Ali let him know that he was a 2 hour drive away from the Queen City. They both was trying to feel each other out, both of them threw numbers in the air but Ali finally said "Anytime you come on my side, I have a 100 grand laying around ready". With that said they exchanged cell numbers with hopes that the other was not bullshitting.

After being in the dog house for a few weeks Isis was still mad at him. He knew that he had to make up big time. The only way he thought he could do that was to buy the biggest gift he could find and at least get a smile from her. Ali was at the Lexus dealership finishing up the paperwork on buying a brand-new Lexus RX 300 SUV. It was so nice and smooth that he thought that he would fuck himself for a gift like this.

Ali pulled up to the apartment he shared with Isis in Westchester Place and went inside. Isis was on the bed feeding the baby. He asked her could he hold and feed his lil man. She sucked her teeth and rolled her eyes, and gave him the baby. After getting the baby he asked her could she go out to his car and get some clothes that he got for the baby, after a few mumbling and grumbling she decided she would. As she walked outside, Ali followed her. She didn't see any of his cars so she turned around only to see Ali smiling holding the baby "I love you and sorry, that's your new car". He could see that she was happy so he told her to go ride out and enjoy herself and he would keep the baby. It was like from break ups to make ups. You got to do what you got to do.

CHAPTER 24
APRIL FOOLS, NOW JOKE IS ON YOU

Ali was at his car wash kicking it with a few of his employees. The car wash was doing very well and Ali was glad that he made the good business decision. It kept him busy and out of a lot of bullshit. He was in school, with his own business and that made him feel good about himself. His phone began to ring and he looked at the caller id and saw an unfamiliar number with a weird area code. "Yo Yo" Ali answered

"You got something for me, I got something for you" the caller said in a Spanish accent. For about a minute Ali was thrown off a little bit because he couldn't figure out who he was speaking with or what the caller was talking about. It wasn't until after the caller said the words Houston, TX that it dawned on Ali who was on the other line. It only took a few minutes to know that Ali amigo friend was all about business and paid close attention to details because not only was the Mexican on the east coast, he was in Orangeburg. It didn't take long to make the decision to deal with the Mexican because Ali knew that the Mexican did not come this far to try some fuck shit or to rob him. Ali went to one of his stash houses to grab the cash for the deal and met up with the amigo at the Ruby Tuesday on 601. After sitting down and eating with him and all the Mexican kept saying was Primo this and Primo that, that Ali made that the name for his new plug.

Primo had 5 neatly packaged kilos for Ali to purchase. Primo let him leave with the 5 keys and one of his henchmen so he could check out the work to see the quality of it. Ali and the henchman went to another of Ali stash houses in Eastwood Acres. Ali tested 2 of the 5 and knew that he had yet another drug connect. Primo and Ali sealed the deal that Ali would buy at least 5 keys a week at a set price of 100 grand.

Ali always had a knack of being a people person so it helped him in the drug game with the way he networked. He now had 3 major drug connects and it seemed that he had an unlimited access to work.

April 1st

Ali was on I-26, he just texted Shakira to ask her how to get to her trailer in Swansea. She texted him back to let him know to get off on exit 136 and which way to get to her house. Ali was getting ready to take finals exams at school and to do some make up work. She had been helping him with his school work and now they both had finals to study for. After pulling up to the trailer, he grabbed his laptop and headed into the mobile home. Once inside he was greeted with a beautiful sight. Shakira was dressed in a 2 piece Pocahontas get up. All Ali could do was look and be amazed at how sexy her body was. She had a waist like a wasp and an ass like a horse, flat stomach and perky breast. Shakira could tell that Ali liked what he saw but told him to get ready to work. He couldn't help but to ask "What you got on". She let him know that's how she walks around the house. "Damn, I wished I lived here" he said low.

While sitting on the couch trying to stay focused on his school work, which was hard to do with Shakira having to get up every 5-10 minutes, to check on the spaghetti that she was cooking. And every time she got up Ali took his eyes off his laptop and put them on her fat ass. He thought that he had to get himself some of that or at least try. Hell, Jet stopped talking to him because he thought he fucked her so why not make it true.

Shakira sat back on the couch beside him but this time she put her small feet into his lap. That instantly got his dick hard as a brick. He lost all focus on his schoolwork and now was thinking of getting some of this sexy chocolate thing. He started rubbing her feet and she had no objection to that so with every circular motion his hands went further and further up her legs. After he got around her thick thighs he could feel the heat coming from her sex box. He opened her legs and could tell that she was more than ready because her wetness was soaking thru her panties. He asked her for a kiss and they began to tongue kiss and he slipped his finger on the inside of her panties into her very warm pussy.

After about 5 minutes of foreplay, Shakira told Ali to sit up straight on the couch. She unbuckled his pants and pulled them down to his ankles and took her panties off and sat down backwards slowly on Ali's dick. He had to fight the urge to bust a nut because of the tightness of her pussy and the feeling of her fat soft ass going up and down on him. She then bent over and grabbed his ankles and started pussy popping on his dick. He knew it was about to be over and he was going to come so he told her and asked did she want him to pull out. Her response was sitting back up straight and squeezing her ass cheeks tight and grinding on his dick using her pussy muscles to squeeze and pull his dick. He couldn't take it no more and came deep inside her.

After cleaning themselves up and getting dressed. He told her "I'm going to make you mine" and she responded "Boy by". He thought this was a good April Fool's day but the joke wasn't on him. LOL

CHAPTER 25

IF IT AINT FOREIGN ITS BORING

JUNE 2006
DISNEY WORLD ORLANDO FLORIDA

Ali was just getting off the plane when he spotted Shakira at the airport waiting on him. Ali thought that he was on a regular vacation because Shakira called him a few days ago, and told him that he need to see him. He thought arrogantly that she must have loved the dick and just wanted some more, because they were fucking on a regular before she went to Orlando on a college intern. The pussy was good to Ali so he just told her to book him a flight. Ali wasn't ready for the news that he got once they made it to the hotel. "Ali, I'm pregnant" she told him. He was taking it in and was like 'ok'.

Shakira was telling Ali about how she was in school and a lot other bullshit that he wasn't trying to hear. He didn't believe in abortions and was sticking to that. After about 30 minutes of arguing he got frustrated and gave her the money and let her know if she wanted to do that, she was going to do it by herself. She went and had the abortion and he told her that he wasn't fucking with her no more, but the pussy was so good he knew that it would be hard but he was glad she was in Orlando so that she could stay the fuck from around him. Killing his kids like that, what the fuck she was thinking about.

Ali was leaving the the Jamison Inn meeting with Ned to get 5 keys, he was out on federal bond but Ali still fucked with Ned because he knew Ned wouldn't cross him out, they both was about making paper. Ali decided to stop by Hibbets Sports to buy some of the new Jordan's that came out. While walking in the store he bumps into Ricky, they give each other dap and proceeded into the store. Once inside the store Rickey started telling Ali about the up-coming Mayweather and Zab Juda fight in Vegas. Ali told him to book the flight because he was going. On the way out the store Ali gave Ricky the keys to his Cadillac and told him to look on the back seat. Ricky eyes lit up when he looked in the bag on the back seat and saw the kilos just sitting there. He got out the car quickly and said that he was wild for riding like that. Ali told him to "Fuck with your boy". He was asking Ricky what he wanted but he kept saying that he was alright. Ali didn't think nothing of so he jumped in the caddy and went to his stash house.

As Ali was at the stash house breaking down the keys and putting them into separate bags for his different customers, he was thinking and he couldn't get out of his head why Ricky wouldn't fuck with him. Ali kept saying to him-self that he knew he had good work and great prices but Ricky was very hesi-tant to fuck with him. It finally dawned on him what the problem was. Ali had a bad reputation as being a jack boy and Ricky wasn't trying to fuck with him like that. So he came up with a remedy for that.

After he finished serving his customers he grabbed a brick and headed to-wards Bayne St. Ali was in his brand-new Ford F-150 pickup truck so no one would recognize him. He called Rickey and told he was about to pull up on him. Once he got to the spot Ricky was already outside so he rolled the win-dow down and told him to jump in with him. Once he got into the truck Ali reached in the middle console and took the brick out and gave it to him. "You can get this for 23 grand cash now, or you can give me 24 grand after you finish it". Ricky hesitated for a minute and then said "I don't have money like that"

"Well do what you do and bring me 24 back, I aint tripping, hit me when you finish". At the time, Rickey was in need of some work and his usual peeps had fell off so he could really could use the kilo in his hand. Ricky ended up taking the kilo to check it out to see if it was good or not and told Ali he would call him in a few to let him know what it was.

About an hour later Rickey called Ali to come thru Bayne St so he could holla at him. When he pulled up to Ricky's grandmother's house, Rickey handed Ali $23,000 cash. Ali knew that Rickey was straight with money so he let him know that he had work, kept work and that he had the best numbers in the city.

On Two Notch road, again, Ali was looking to purchase another vehicle. This time he was looking for a toy for himself. His birthday was in a few weeks and he couldn't figure out what he wanted to buy himself for his special day. Ali wanted to change the game up in his city and get something that nobody else had. Ali noticed that his pussy rate went up when he copped the Lexus for Isis, so he knew that he would be going foreign this time. His favorite saying was going to be "If it ain't foreign it's boring".$63,000 dollars later, Ali was on the interstate with a 2006 midnight blue 745i with the butter guts (interior). On I-26 headed to Orangeburg he spotted another 745 and decided to ride up on it. When he got bumper to bumper with the other beemer he looked at the driver and noticed it was a female driving it. He nodded his head at the driver, feeling himself like yeah bitch, I'm riding big too. The female driver looked at him and gave him a facial expression that said "Are you serious" and stepped on the gas and pulled away from Ali shaking her head and laughing. As she was passing him, he noticed that her Beemer said 745Li on the back. He knew that he had to see what that meant.

CHAPTER 26
"IMAGINARY PLAYERS" JAY Z

After Ali got off the interstate he went straight to one of his stash houses and got on the internet and looked up the BMW website. Instantly Ali felt stupid and the song by Jay Z "Imaginary Players" came to mind. Stupid nigga wanted to know what's the difference between the 745i and the 745Li. 10-20 grand! Fuck that, I got to upgrade. 3 days later, he copped the 2006 metallic gray 745Li with all black interior. He knew exactly what he was going to do with the other one.

At Club U Neek for Ali birthday bash, he was feeling like new money. He did it again this year, he rented out the whole club and everything was free. Free admission, free drinks and free food. O-Zone came up from Miami and told Ali that the Cubans sent 5 bricks up for him, so he felt even better knowing that he was going to make the money back that he spent that week. He was enjoying himself and talking to all the niggas that he did business with and all them needed to be supplied. He counted that all the bricks that he had would be gone the next day. The club was filled with a bunch of chicks who were dressed to impress and he was flirting and fucking with all of them. When he was taking pictures somebody asked him why he didn't get one of the new charges he yelled "If it aint foreign, it's boring".

August 2006
Montego Bay, Jamaica

O-Zone and his wife invited Ali and Isis on a trip with them to Jamaica. They were staying at the Half Moon Resort at one of the villas on the island being treated like kings and queens. They had maids, butlers, chiefs and drivers. Ali only could think, this is what money could do. Apples and Isis was on a spa day getting pampered, while O-Zone and Ali chopped it up about some things that was going on. O-Zone began telling Ali that the price of coke was going up and that a drought maybe coming up around the same time. O-Zone was just like a stock broker and always thought about the future and was always staying ahead of the game. Ali took it all in but wasn't thinking about it too much. He knew as long as he got the drugs that he could make anything happen.

As Ali and O-Zone is talking his phone rings, but being in another country the phone was roaming and the call came up unavailable. "Who dis"

"That's how you doing it?" The caller said. He started smiling because he knew who the caller was and what she was talking about.

"Yeah I just upgraded you" Ali said. Sherina was over excited and Ali swore he could see her smiling thru the phone.

"Where you at so I can suck that lil dick"

"I thought you never did that before"

"I never did but I'm going to try something new on you"

"Damn, if I would have known that I would have been upgraded you" Ali says with a big laugh. They talked on the phone for about 20 minutes about the 745i that he sent over to the Cayman Island and how all her coworkers were sweating her new ride. Sherina really wanted to get up with Ali and was willing to jump on a flight that day but he let her know that he was in Jamaica and would be back in a week. So they made plans for her to book him a flight when he got back to the states, so he could come over and she could give him a ride around the island in her new whip, ride him both ways she said.

Sept. 2006
Untouchable Hands Car Wash

Ali had just pulled back up to his car wash after selling a half of kilo to one of his customers from Kingstree SC. He sat in his car counting the $11,500 to make sure it was all there so he could take it to one of his stash houses later. DT, his head employee came over to the F150 and asked Ali did he want his truck washed and Ali said yeah and got out and let the crew do what they do. While they were washing his truck, DT told Ali that the word around the city was that he rented the 745Li that he had on his bday. All Ali could do was laugh because he knew that the city wasn't ready for that type shit nor could they believe that Ali was doing numbers like that. "Oh yeah, they think I rented the car"

"I told them fuck niggas that my boss man can buy anything that he wants, they just hating is all." DT said

The next day Ali was at Salter's body shop talking to Johnny. He was in need for something exotic to paint the car. Ali was going to go with a candy paint job but Johnny showed him some new paint that came out called Hot Hues. He decided to go with the Fuchsia Kiss color and left the Beemer and 10 grand cash to be painted and put first in line.

A week later Ali was driving thru town in his newly painted Beemer. The sun was beaming all over the quarter to eight and the shit was shining. He could see that paint job was a real neck breaker and was getting all the attention. He had dark tint on the car so nobody knew it was him. He was even getting calls from folks all around the 'Dirty Burg' telling him that somebody had a whip like his but had a bad paint job on it. They were suggesting to him that he should paint his car like he did the truck. He was playing right along with them telling them that he would think about it.

Ali pulled up to the car wash and all his employees stopped what they were doing to watch the shiny new car pull up. When he jumped out the car, all his employee's eyes got big and their smiles got even bigger on their faces. All of them came over and gave their approval of the boss's car. He pulled out four $100 bills and gave one to each of his workers and told them to wash one of the 22'inch Divinci rims but told them "Don't touch the car, that shit still wet" laughing. "Tell them niggas, you don't paint no rental"

Chapter 27

Jack Pot

Shakira's Trailer, Swansea SC

Ali was getting ready to do the biggest deal that he ever did. O-Zone had the Cubans to sell him 10 kilos for 18 grand a piece. Earlier he had given Shakira a duffle bag full of money to count and vacuum seal for him.

"Puddin Butt, how much money was it" Ali asks her.

"180 thousand"

They began to put 3 stacks of 10 grand a piece in bags to be vacuums sealed. He let her know that he was going to be out of town for a few days but when he returned he wanted to get up with her and do something nice. She said that it was ok but told him that they couldn't meet up there anymore. He didn't really care one way or another but he did like fucking her every chance he got. "I told you to get your own place anyway". They discussed for a few minutes on where they would hook up after he got back.

Miami, Fl.

O-Zone and Ali was at the motel on South Beach waiting to meet up with the connect. They usually dealt with the older Cuban named Miguel but Miguel usually took 2-3 month vacation during the year. He used to say that he would hustle for 3 months and take 3 months off. So now that he was out of town O-Zone was dealing with Jose, which was Miguel nephew. Jose was very flashy, arrogant and wild. "What time they going to show up" Ali asked.

"I don't know but they were supposed to be here about an hour ago". The kicked it in the room for a few more minutes then decided to go grab something to eat. Ali didn't like the way the motel was set up so he grabbed the duffel bag to take with them.

Once outside, as they walk towards the rented Chrysler 300 they see a cripple guy hobbling along on some crutches. Ali told O-Zone to pop the trunk so he could put the bag inside. After he hit the button on the key ring and the trunk came up. Ali was just about to put the bag in the trunk when the cripple guy crept up from behind him, only now the cripple guy didn't have the crutches in his hands, he now had a mini assault rifle pointed at them.

"Give that shit up, don't make me kill yall" the robber said with a Spanish accent. All kind of thoughts are going thru Ali's head. He didn't know if he wanted to buck the jack and fight for his money or make a run for it. Ali looked into the robber's eyes and from one killer to another, he could tell that he was about his business, so held the bag out for the robber to take. The robber then made them empty their pockets and take off all their jewelry they had on. After getting everything, the robber then zipped open the bag to put everything he had taken inside and seen all the money and said "Jack Pot". He then made O-Zone and Ali turn and walk the other way.

On the way back home Ali was damn near in tears thinking about what had just taken place. He didn't know if he was in so much pain because of the money he lost, or that he felt like a pussy for not putting up a fight or how stupid he felt for getting robbed. Ali thought it was a set up from the Cubans but O-Zone didn't think it was them. His way of thinking was the Cubans had plenty of money and drugs and that was petty for them. Either way Ali was out of 180 stacks and made a promise to himself that he would not go out like that again. The only good thing that O-Zone said "It's better to leave with your life, than to die with your money"

December 2006
Club Tunnel, Holly Hill SC

Ali and O-Zone was inside of this new club getting their party on. One of Ali new customers told him about the club and it was just as advertised. It was super pack and filled with bad bitches from that area, Charleston and Sumter

SC. O-Zone came down to talk to Ali about getting some more businesses and to try to get him to move out of Orangeburg. "Ali listen to me, you have outgrown Orangeburg, it's time to move out the city." He went on to tell Ali that with the money he had he could move wherever he wanted and that he had a target on his back from the jack boys, local Narcs, DEA and the haters. "You have blown past all them niggas down there, you fucking all their bitches and you making all the money, them niggas can't take that". He was trying to get Ali to see that all the niggas he came up with and hustle with wasn't on his level and some niggas didn't know how to deal with that.

After the last setback, Ali took he went even harder in the streets, breaking down every brick he had and catching every sale he could. Ali had gotten a big chunk of the money back that he lost but was still going hard in the paint.

"Ali what do you see when you come out your apartment" Ozone asked Ali.

"I see all my cars"

"You know what I see, I see over a $150 thousand dollar worth of cars in front of an apartment" O-Zone says seriously. After that Ali realizes that it didn't make sense to have 2-3 hundred thousand dollars worth of cars, something that loses value every year and not have a house of your own. He said in 2007 he was going to move out of Orangeburg and get him a big house somewhere. As they chopped it up about what kind of shit they would get into that year, Ali spotted his new customer 'Money'. Money was from Santee and was doing numbers down there. O-Zone and Money grandfather use to get money back in the days before they both caught fed time. Ali pointed Money out to O-Zone and let him know "That kid right there got this area on lock down, he moving them things like water" After Ali explained who he was, O-Zone said "It's in his blood, his granddaddy was a go getter, you need to lock him in"

"I already did" and they both laughed

As they partied in the V.I.P section Ali saw Tina out on the floor wearing some stilettos but was dancing like she had on sneakers. Ali was mesmerized by the way Tina was working her hips and throwing her fat ass from side to side. Ali got her attention and then let security know to let her come thru. They both started flirting and smiling at each other as soon as they got close to one another. "Can I go home with you tonight?" Ali said jokingly but was very serious. "Yep, I aint got no boyfriend no more" Tina lets Ali know.

"I seen you dancing over there"

"I know you was watching me" Tina says with a smile

"I bet you can't do that with a dick in you"

"I can do that and more" Tina says deviously. Tina was getting Ali super excited and hard so they decided to exit the club and take it to a room. And when they got to the Days Inn off Hwy 301, Tina did not disappoint. She had Ali to cum about 3 times with all the positions they did that night. Each time he came harder inside of Tina.

CHAPTER 28
MILLION DOLLAR DREAMS

"I Ain't Begging I'm Buying"
Jan 2007, Westchester Apartments

Ali was sitting in his room watching First 48 while counting money. He was thinking what all he wanted to accomplish this year. First, he wanted to buy a big house worth at least a quarter million. He also wanted to be a millionaire by his 26th birthday. He wanted to have a million in cash and not include cars and houses. He was thinking it should come together because he had a lot of different plugs (drug connections) and plenty clientele to purchase the work once he got it. Ali had gotten back stronger then he was before he took that last 180 grand loss. He also stepped his game up to he only re-up with 10 kilos at a time. Ali said from that point he would not break any kilos down, if you copped from him you had to buy a whole one, nothing less. Ali wasn't paying no more than 20 grand a piece for the bricks and since he was buying the bricks upfront they gave him front door service. Ali had to think back when he had Ned to go to Gizmo to buy the 10 bricks and Gizmo had some of his crew with him and they were feeling some type way because Ali was much younger than they were and he was getting way more money than them. On top of that Ali wanted to get the bricks for 20 stacks a piece, when they were paying $23,000 to $24,000 a block. Ned came back and said that the niggas was saying that Ali was trying to get the dope for free and that he was begging. Ned told Ali that most of them was getting 1 to 2 bricks at a time and it was being fronted to them. Ali thought about it for a second and gave Ned the bag with

200 grand cash and said tell them niggas "I aint begging, I'm buying". Twenty minutes later Ned came back with the 10 bricks and said Gizmo was not about to pass up that cash money up.

Later on that night, Ali ended up with Ice and his Ice's girlfriend who was a realtor with Exit Real Estate company. Ice had gotten himself a big house out in the Summit, and Ali wanted to get a big house in Columbia, the capitol of South Carolina. Ice girlfriend knew what kind of dude Ali was so her only question was "How much money you trying to spend?"

"200, no more than a quarter"

CHAPTER 29
ALI'S ALL-STAR TEAM

Feb 2007

NBA All-Star Weekend, Las Vegas Nevada

Ali and Ricky was checking into the MGM Grand Hotel for this years NBA All-Star festivities. This was Ali 5th time coming to Las Vegas but the first time bringing a female companion. Ali didn't gamble nor did he trick with the local prostitutes. Over in Vegas, selling pussy was legal but he wasn't feeling that because he liked to fuck raw and he couldn't do that with a trick. So he ended up bringing Holiday, a bartender from the Club Tunnel with him to enjoy the weekend.

"What's up Puddin Butt" Ali answered the phone.

"I have something to tell you" Shakira responded.

"Well tell me then"

"Ali, I'm pregnant". Ali didn't know what to say, this was the second call he got since he was in Vegas. In both conversation, it was about a pregnancy. Tina had called and let him know that she was pregnant with her first child and that Ali was that father. Now Shakira was telling him she was pregnant again. He thought about the last time Shakira was pregnant and she had the abortion. "What the fuck you telling me for, I aint killing no kids"

"I wasn't calling you to tell you that stupid, I was calling to tell you that I'm keeping my baby." Ali smiled and told her he would get up with her when he got back to South Carolina. Ali didn't know what he was going to do but shit was about to hit the fan with his love life. Isis was about to have their second child any day now. With Shakira and Tina pregnant that made 6 kids for him. All he could say was "Ali love the kids"

Ali, Ricky, Holiday and Ashley were at the All-Star game inside the UNLV stadium. They were watching the East and West coast all-stars play their game and put on for the crowd. This gave Ali time to reflect on his drug business. He easily compared his drug dealing with players on the basketball court. He had a starting 5 players that could go against any team. Ali had Fat Boy starting at center and he was like Shaq in his prime. He had Ricky at power forward and he was like Dirk Nowinski. He had Lil Blue from Norway at shooting guard and he was like a young Kobe Bryant . He had Money from Santee at point guard and he was like Allen Iverson in his prime. Ali was at small forward and he was Lebron James, he could play any position on the court because he was just like that. Ali thought about his team and about all the bricks they were selling in the city and knew that nobody was fucking with them.

CHAPTER 30
"MAYBE YOU WILL KNOW MONEY WHEN YOU SEE MONEY"

March 2007
Aun and McCay Law Office, Columbia SC

Ali was signing the paper work and gave the lawyer who was doing the deal for his real estate purchase a cashier check for $225,000. He was now the owner of a 3,500-square foot two story house in Irmo SC, in the Misty Glen subdivision. He was feeling beyond great because of his first residence. He decided that he would go out later that night to celebrate his success

After he returned from Las Vegas, all hell broke loose. Somehow Isis, Shakira and Tina talked and everybody knew he had gotten all of them pregnant. Isis had given birth a few weeks prior but that wasn't the reason he wasn't getting no play. Isis, Tina and Shakira would give Ali no pussy because he was fucking the others. Ali even tried his usual and went and purchased a brand-new candy apple red Cadillac SUV for Isis, but she still wouldn't give him no play. Even Rashawn wasn't fucking with him, he copped her the new X-type Jaguar but she was fucking with him either. All he could do was shake his head and think about what was going on. He was like fuck it and went to celebrate the success of getting a new house.

Club Diamonds

Ali was in Club Diamonds popping X pills and drinking Moet feeling on top of the world. He was buying drinks and showing everybody pictures of his new house on his camera phone. He was on his way back to the bar when he spotted this chick in all black. He thought that he recognized her face but couldn't remember where he knew her from. The girl noticed Ali was watching her so she smiled and waved at him. Ali took that as an opening to approach her and when Ali got closer to the chick he was surprised to see who she was. It was Tyler, the little girl that use to walk by his car wash every day to speak to him. Well she use to be little girl, but she not little no more, and she sure wasn't looking like a little girl that night. She ditched her jeans and Air Force Ones and Jordans for an all black leather skirt and high heels. She had let her hair down and had the grown and sexy look down to the T.

"You didn't know who I was, did you?" a smiling Tyler said

"Naw, I thought you was somebody grown"

"I am grown"

"So what happen"

"What you mean what happen"

"How you got all that" Ali said pointing at Tyler's ass

"I been had this, you never took the time to look"

"You right, I don't be looking at no lil girls"

"I'm not a lil girl, so stop saying that' Lil girls don't have all this" Tyler said and rubbed her ass on Ali's crotch. He had to think about all the times that Tyler use to walk by or stop by his car wash and he just paid her no mind because he thought she was too young.

"Are you old enough to drink?"

"I'm in the club aint I?" Ali just smiled and asked her what she was drinking.

"Whatever you drinking". With that Ali got another bottle of Moet and they drinked it together, the whole time Ali was just looking Tyler up and down.

"You keep looking at me like you want some of this" Tyler said

"I do"

"You can have it if you want it". That was all that needed to be said. They exited the club and jumped in the 745 and headed up 601....

Ali was half wake and half sleep with all kind of thoughts in his head. Ali was thinking about the dream he had last night. It was of him in Club Diamonds and he ran across Tyler, the girl from around the corner from his car wash. Ali was smiling to himself because in the dream he had a very explicit sexual encounter with her. She was more than a woman the way she handled herself in the bedroom with him. When Ali finally woke completely up, he couldn't believe what position he was in. Ali was buck naked and Tyler was laying on top of him and his dick was still inside of her. What Ali thought was a drunken stupor was real life. Tyler little short ass rode him to sleep, well they both was knocked the fuck out. He decided to take advantage of his morning hard on and started moving his hips to see if he could get a reaction out of Tyler. After a few thrust he could hear her starting to moan and the started to get in the mood just as well. He couldn't accept the fact that he went to sleep the night before, so he was going to take full control this time and put it down. He flipped her over and did a few shallow strokes before going long and hard. Tyler whispered to Ali "You know we did it all last night, right?"

"We did?" Ali asked surprised

"I'm a lil sore right now"

"You want me to stop?"

"No, you can have this pussy if you want". Ali started pounding harder after that. She was about to cum he figured because she started moaning "Pussy don't fail me now". A few minutes later they both came in unison.

After dropping Tyler off, Ali headed to Columbia to do some shopping for his new house. He needed all new everything. He decided to go on Harbison Blvd to the Rooms 2 Go store. As he walked in he tried to get the attention of a black store clerk, while doing so the clerk was half as helping him and decided that Ali wasn't that important and went to help another customer. After walking around the huge store, he was approached by a younger white female clerk that asked if he needed help. "I want some of the best furniture that you have here." The white chick wasn't sure of what he wanted or what his financial status was but she was willing to share her time and help him out. Ali picked out furniture for every room in his house. "I want all those that I picked out" he let the clerk know.

"What will be your method of payment sir?"

"CASH!". Ali went back to the car and grabbed a black Coogi bag and went straight to the counter. His total was almost 50 grand. As the white girl was counting out the money, the black guy that brushed him off earlier heard about what was going on and tried to talk to Ali and speak some black helping blacks type shit, but Ali stopped him dead in his tracks and let him k now how he tried to fuck with the "Black Man" and he chumped him off like he was window shopper. "Kick rocks nigga, maybe next time you will know money when you see money"

After leaving Rooms 2 Go, Ali headed to Best Buy to get some tv's for his house. Flat screens were just hitting the market and he had to have all the new shit. In Best Buy, he was like a kid in a candy store with all the electronics. He got flat screens for every room in the house, new front loader washer and dryer but what set it off was the new refrigerator with the flat screen built in it that had just come out. With Ali, he had to stunt so he copped that also.

As he got on to I-26 to head back to Orangeburg, Ali spotted the Infiniti dealership. He had really been digging that new QX56 truck and wanted to get an up-close look and feel of it. He knew he shouldn't stop because he knew if he liked it he was going to buy it. And just as he thought, he liked it and had to have it. He test drove a champagne gold one with the butter guts (interior) with the maple oak wood grain. He let the car salesman know he would be back the next day to get it.

Chapter 31
"Men Lie, Women Lie, Numbers Don't"

BACK ON DA GRIND

Ali pulled up on State Court to the trap spot that C-Lo was running. Ali just purchased 10 bricks from Yvonne and was ready to get rid of them. As he walked into the mobile home he could see that it was a full house. He sat the bag down on the kitchen table and asked Malcom could he go around to his house and get his money counter.

As Malcom was leaving his brother Tank came out of one of the back rooms, drunk as usual. Tank started off talking slick. Ever since Tank started hustling on Aaron street for Jet he was thinking he was big shit. "You still got that bullshit dope?" he said referring to Ali.

"I got the best shit in town nigga" Ali just laughed at him for how silly he sounded. "You fuck around and I make sure your boss man and his boss man don't get no dope"

"Fuck you mean"

"I mean I supply the city, that's what the fuck I mean"

"You aint working with nothing but a brick nigga"

"A brick, nigga I count in tens, if you aint got 10, don't talk to me"

"You faking nigga". The exchange back and forth was getting Ali hyped up. He never showed a nigga what he was working with but Tank had gotten under his skin. He wanted him to know just who he was fucking with.

"Yall niggas getting 4 ½ together over there, yall aint getting no money"

"Our trap bumping way harder than what you doing" Tank said with a serious face and tone

Ali laughed and said "I bet I will sell 20 bricks tonight and let you see me count the money"

"Nigga stop with all that flawging"

With that being said, Ali started calling up all his customers and let them know he was ready for business. Ali knew that he only had 10 bricks so he called Ice to see if they were on deck. After getting confirmation that Gizmo was on deck, Ali was about to let the money do the talking. He took the 10 blocks out the bag and placed them on the table and said "Let me show you how to get some real money, matter of fact you better see if your boss man need some dope before I sell it all" laughing. Fat Boy came and got 3, Money came and got 3 and Ricky got the last 4. Every time Ali sold some work he would let Tank know what the count was. Once he got the money he let Tank two brothers count the money. The whole time Fred and Malcom was singing "We getting money over here"! Tank was still hating and said that was only 10.

"Just keep counting, I'm about to get 10 more, and if anybody know somebody that need dope and their money right, tell them shop open". Ali left and met Ice and got the 10 bricks and headed back to State Court. Ali had his customers coming thru with stacks of money. Chin's girlfriend asked Ali did he have any extra work to sell because she knew somebody that wanted one. "Yeah, I got one, who want it?"

"Fat Boy off Stilton" Tina said. The Dash Street crew wasn't having that and convinced Ali not to sell to them niggas. They wanted to keep the spot bumping and selling to the competition would just slow the money up. Ali shrugged his shoulders and said "My dawgs said no, so I can't sell them none." After selling 18 of the 20, Ali let C-Lo and the Thomas boys break the other 2 bricks down. Tank was still drunk but Ali knew that he was amazed at what he just saw. "I'm about to get my bitch and go home, but remember this 'MEN LIE, WOMEN LIE, NUMBERS DON'T!" Ali said before walking outside.

CHAPTER 32
DIAMONDS ARE A GIRL BEST FRIEND

Atlantic City, NJ

Ali was standing behind Shakira rubbing her stomach while they both were looking out the large window at the ocean. Shakira was about 5 months pregnant and showing very well now. Even though Shakira was pregnant with Ali's child, she was still in a so-called relationship with Jet. He figured that she was just confused and did not want to let go of the past. It was her spring break from school, so he asked her where she wanted to go on vacation since this was her last spring break before she graduated from SCSU with a bachelor degree in business. He wanted to make her his main chick because he could see that she wanted something out of life. They had not spoken for about 2 months because they had a big falling out behind Ali wanting her to himself and Shakira having a strong minded attituded wanting to do what she wanted to do. That didn't matter thou, because as soon as he called, Shakira booked the flight and here they were, looking out at the ocean looking like a happy couple.

"Ali, you coming to my graduation?"

"If your boyfriend doesn't come, I will be there"

"You better be there too"

Ali moved his hands down into Shakira's panties and started playing with her clit. She responded by grinding her fat ass on his dick. After about 5 minutes of rubbing her clit, he pulled his dick out and entered her from the back. She bent slightly over and grabbed the balcony as Ali took slow long strokes while squeezing her soft ass cheeks. Their movements were in unison with the ocean as the could hear as the waves came in. It was people on the beach 15 floors down but it didn't matter because they were oblivious to what was going on up there and they were in another world rocking to the beat of the ocean.

Atlanta GA,
Magic City strip club

"You need to invest your money in some diamonds, they never lose value" Dooley tells Ali. Dooley was a Jamaican connect for Gemini that supplied him with weed. He was real major in that game and invited Gemini and Ali down to the CTE "Coldest Summer Ever" album release party. Dooley was real cool with Kinky B, so they all was V.I.P for the night. He was rocking a chain and charm with black diamonds in them. Ali was soaking up a little game and trying to really see the point. He had a pocket full of money and was ready to act a fool. But for some reason the hoes wasn't even fucking with Ali. All the strippers were on Kinky B and Dooley and they weren't spending money. Ali had on the big dope boy chain but it didn't have diamonds on it. Every time Ali looked in Kinky B and Dooley direction he could see the different color lights bouncing off their jewelry.

After leaving Magic City, the entourage headed to Body Taps. Kinky B was in the cocaine white Porsche Cayenne Super Sport, Dooley was in the all white Range Rover Super Charged and Ali was his Beemer. As they walked down the stairs to the main part of the club, Ali saw the most strippers he seen in his life at one time. It seemed like every one of them was super thick just like he liked them. "How much these hoes charge in here?" Ali asks Dooley.

"The price of pussy is high in here tonight."

"We got plenty of money" Ali says grabbing his overstuffed pockets.

"You see who in here? Them hoes ain't fucking with us until they strike out" Dooley says pointing towards the stage

"Who that is"

"Allen Iverson and Jermaine Dupree". Dooley let him know but didn't have to point out which one they were. Because the both of them had on jewelry that was catching all the lights and had all the bitches sweating them. 'Diamonds are a girl's best friend!!'

The same day Ali got back to South Carolina he went to Columbia Mall to talk to his jeweler A.J. that had a store across from Foot Action and Lim's.

"I want something that's going to catch all the lights" Ali tells A.J.

"Well you going to need good diamonds for that" A.J. lets him know and went on to tell Ali about the best diamonds and the cut and clarity of them. "You don't want those cloudy diamonds like the ones those guys have in the middle of the mall." They settled on getting some VVS, VS and SI diamonds to be made into a custom-made Shriek chain and charm.

CHAPTER 33
"AINT NO FUN WHEN THE RABBIT GOT THE GUN"

"Yeah, meet me at the Arby's gas station off exit 139" Ali tells Jose thru his Nextel twerp. Pedro was in the area and called Ali the day before and let him know that he had 10 bricks if he wanted them. Not one to turn down a business opportunity and extra money, Ali jumped on the deal. The deal was going to go down at the spot that they handled business at before on previous occasions. Ali had family and property in the Sweet Water Lake area and they were going to get down there.

Ali was sitting in his Infinity truck talking on the phone when Jose pulled up in a black Dodge Ram pickup truck. "What they do" Ali says and give Jose dap thru the window.

"Nothing much, just trying to get back on the road, you ready?" Jose responded like he was in a hurry. Ali was having a bad vibe for like a week or so and now it was getting stronger. Then his focused went on the passenger who was sitting quiet and looking straight forward but avoiding eye contact with him. As Ali was telling Jose to follow him, the hair stood up on the back of his neck. When the passenger lifted his arm to move the visor down, he saw the tattoo. It was the same tattoo of the Cuban flag and a symbol of a Cuban gang under it like the one the robber wore that jacked Ali and O-Zone while they were down in Miami months earlier.

After Ali got back into his SUV, he put the gear in neutral, hit the brakes and turned the radio to a preset station to trigger the stash spot the he had installed in the truck. When it opened, Ali grabbed the Sig Sauer Glock 40 and check to make sure that he had one in the head. He knew what he had to do and what he was going to do. That was take both out the first chance that he got. He wanted to execute them right in the parking lot but knew he would go to jail for it so he decided to go to the spot and handle business.

When they pulled into the yard of the mobile home, Ali jumped out of the truck and headed towards Jose's truck. He motioned for Jose to let his window down, after he did so Ali reached in his pocket and pulled out the Glock 40, reached over Jose and started firing. BANG! BANG! BANG! BANG! BANG! Ali hit the passenger with all 5 shots to the face and side of the head. "Fuck ass nigga, you thought I didn't know it was you" Ali said with venom in his voice. Jose had balled up in the driver seat and was now looking at Ali with fear in his eyes as Ali had the Glock pointed directly in his face. "Where my shit at?" Ali asked

"What are you talking about?" Jose responded weakly trying to play stupid and act like he didn't know what was going on.

"My 180 grand y'all got me for in Miami".

After seeing that Ali wasn't playing and meant business, Jose decided to come clean and try to save his life. He went on to explain that he had fucked up his uncle money and needed a come up but it wasn't his idea, it was the dead passenger's idea. Ali wasn't trying to hear the bullshit or the sob story, he was more concerned about the 10 bricks they were going to sell him. All Ali was getting was more sad stories and excuses. After checking the stash spot and the rest of the truck, he found 2 guns, a little less that a kilo and about 40 grand in cash. He then realized that they were coming to rob and maybe kill him this time so he pointed the gun at Jose's head and said "Ain't no fun when the rabbit got the gun" and shot him twice in the dome.

Ali was in deep thought now because he had 2 dead bodies and a pickup truck on his property that he needed to make disappear. So he called one of his partners that had a back hoe digger. Candy Man answered and came over to help him out. He was an ex-hustler from Miami who now had several legit businesses. Candy Man unhooked the GPS for the Dodge Ram and dug a hole big enough for the truck to go into. Ali pushed the truck with the dead bodies into the hole and Candy Man covered it up. He gave Candy Man 10 grand for his trouble and just like that, his problem was solved.

CHAPTER 35
Million Dollar Dreams
And Federal Nightmares

July 2007

"Hey, you coming over for my party?" Ali asks Sherina over the cellphone.

"I want too but you not going to have no time for me, you got too many bitches that's going to want your attention."

"Well how about you book us a trip to the Bahamas and we stay at the Atlantis" Ali suggested

"You love that resort, don't you?"

"You already know, it's beautiful and relaxing". They made plans to hook up after his b-day party at their favorite spot. He also got confirmation on what he already knew. Ali was now officially a millionaire. Not property, cars or assets but a million dollars in cash. With the money he had in his account in the Cayman Island and his money he had in the States, Ali did what most drug dealers dreamed of. It was not a dream or imagination anymore, it was now reality. The kid did it, he made a dream come true.

Once he got off the phone with Sherina, he sat and contemplated what he was going to do next. He had it all, money, houses, cars, and women. It was nothing that he wanted that he didn't have. He still was in deep thought thou. His mind flashed back to the last two clowns that he gave a dirt nap too. He knew sooner or later that he would have to put his murder game down when a nigga got out of line or tried his gangsta behind this drug game. It's part of the game, he knew that already. So it was nothing else to do or no other choice to make but to leave the game. Ali was going to retire from the game while he was on top. He was going to retire at the age of 25.

He decided that he wasn't going to tell anyone until his birthday party that it was over with. He knew that it would hurt his clientele to know they would have to find a new plug but he just had to exit the game. But being the stunner that he was, he had to go out with a bang. He had really been jocking the new 2007 650i BMW and he just had to have it. It had a price ticket of $89,000 but fuck it, what was a 100 grand to a millionaire, he laughed and thought to himself. He also wanted to show his loyalty and appreciation to the block, so he bought a house on Dash Street. $150 grand later, Ali had his birthday presents.

Club U Neek
July 31st

Ali did it big once again. Rented the club out, free drinks, free food, free admission and the city came out to show love. Ali was just enjoying himself, mingling in the club and drinking and having a ball. He stepped outside to use the phone. "Make sure my Angel be wake when I come by tonight" Ali told Tina, she gave birth to child a few weeks prior.

"She going to be up and she hungry too, she wants steak, eggs and pancakes from IHOP" Tina says.

Ali looks at the phone strange and says "She aint but 3 weeks old, she can't eat steaks?

"I know but her mommy does" Tina laughs

"I got you, I will be there after the club". He disconnects as he sees Ricky approaching. "What's up my dude" they embrace each other with a hug and dap.

"Tell me it ain't so?" Ricky asks Ali

"What's that?"

"That you retired"

"Yeah man, I got to give it up"

"I ain't mad at you, you did it all"

"Thanks, I respect you for that". They chopped it up for a few more minutes and headed back into the club.

CHAPTER 36
"NEVER CHANGE" JAY-Z

August 2007

About a week or so into his retirement, Ali got a call he was dreading but half ass expected. He had already told O-Zone that he was throwing the towel in and calling it quits. O-Zone respected him for his decision and thought it was a good idea. He called Ali earlier and was like Miquel wanted to have a conversation with him. Ali was skeptical about it because he had murdered his nephew a few months prior and wondered was he wanting revenge. Even though the bodies have not been discovered, he still was a little weary about this so called conversation. The only thing that eased his mind a little bit was the fact that he got to choose where they could talk, Ali chose Dash Street.

Ali was sitting on the porch of the house he purchased when O-Zone pulled up. Ali jumped off the porched and greeted him with pounds and daps. They talked for a few minutes about what was going on in the hood and the city before Ali asked what was this so called meeting was about. O-Zone let him know that he ended up telling Miquel about him retiring and that Miquel just wanted to see if he could get one of his best customers back. Ali reiterated that it was over and he was out of the game but O-Zone convinced him to hear the Cuban out.

Miquel pulled up in an all black Yukon Denali and got out the back seat. He approached O-Zone and Ali, the whole time Ali was checking out his movements and demeanor. As Miquel gave both handshakes and hugs, Ali looked in his eyes to see if he seen any kind of negative vibes but could not detect any. After a few minutes of shit talking, Miquel asked could they walk a little so they could talk more privately.

As they were walking down Dash St, Miquel wasted no time getting to the point. "Why you cut me off like that?" he asked in his deep Cuban accent

"I decided to leave the game alone, I achieved the goal I set out to get, so it's over" Ali explained to him.

"What, are the prices to high?"

"Naw, you have good prices"

"Work no good?"

"Naw the work good, every time A-1 shit, no problems"

"So you make a lot of money and you sell no more?"

"Yeah man, get out while I'm ahead".

Miquel just shook his head and smiled as if he agreed and understood. Then the conversation took an awkward turn because Miquel started doing all the talking.

"You buy 40 to 50 kilos every month. I can count on that. You make me a lot of money, I will miss you a whole lot. I would be ok if my nephew Jose sell a lot of drugs for me, make me a lot of money. But we can't find Jose, he just gone". Ali just listened and kept his stride without even a blink or flinch.

Miquel went on to tell Ali that he would send 50 keys at a time and store them in a storage unit and when Ali would call he would send somebody up to come serve him. Then after Jose went "missing" he just sent 100 kilos up to South Carolina because he knew that Ali could move them. Then he got the call from O-Zone that Ali retired and now he had 100 kilos and a nephew missing and nobody to move them. Ali felt like it was a light press game but Jose said something that made him feel as if it was more of a favor than any-thing else. "I give you the keys to the storage and you sell them how you want to sell them, it's a major drought, I give them to you for 22 grand a piece". Ali took the keys to the storage unit and was thinking that he could sell each brick for 25 grand easily because of the drought and that he did not have to pay for the drugs upfront. He couldn't lose with that, so he agreed.

"You a good guy, if you ever need a favor, call me" Miquel said

After Miquel pulled off, O-Zone asked Ali "What was the verdict?"

"I guess I'm out of retirement for a while" Ali laughed and told him what was going on.

August 29th

Ali was feeling great today. He just left Shakira's house on Bayne Street after playing with his son that she gave birth too. He was happy about that but more overjoyed about the fact he had put a dent in the 100 bricks that was left for him. He was heading up the North Rd to the storage facility to get 3 bricks for Fat Boy. Ali was feeling real coopish, so he had the drop top beemer out with the top peeled back playing Jay-Z greatest hit cd with the song 'Never Change' pumping to the max.

Seawright Street.

Fat boy was chilling waiting on Ali to arrive to bring him the 3 bricks that he ordered, he had 5 recompress machines and a 5-gallon bucket of the cut called 'Miami Ice'. He was ready to get down to business but unbeknownst to him, he was under surveillance and had a tracking device on his car and his every move was being monitored. He sold to a confidential informant in Myrtle Beach, South Carolina and they attached a GPS box on his car when he went to the Waffle House after the sale. They were aiming to catch him in Myrtle Beach but he never came back or so they thought, Fat Boy was in Myrtle Beach everyday but he had a few cars so he rarely drove the Dodge Magnum that had the GPS attached to it. So Ali was driving into a spider web that was going to be hell getting out of.

As Ali and Fat Boy was in the house cooking up dope and counting money, the local narcotics agents were in deep conversation about what was going on. They just observed Ali pull up in a brand-new BMW but did now know who the driver was. Ali nor Fat Boy was on the local radar because they did not sell much drugs in the city or have a trap house or anything to link them too. The narcs did not know what to do because they did not know if there were drugs in the house and there was no traffic coming or going. After about 45 minutes, Ali emerged from the mobile home and hopped into his Beemer and sped out of the yard. The narcotic agents wanted to see who was in the BMW so they decided to initiate a traffic stop.

Ali turned left onto Goff Avenue and punched the gas as he listened to 'Never Change'. He had the 75 grand sitting on the passenger side seat and turned on Coleman Avenue to ride thru the block. When he hit the corner, he noticed a white guy driving a gray 2005 Chevy Impala. He decided not to stop by Whoodie and Ice spot and kept going to turn onto 601. As he sat at the end of Coleman he saw that the Impala was still behind him. He was thinking who could it be, it could be the Feds or it could just be an insurance man. If it was the Feds, he was hit because they had to know that he just sold 3 bricks to Fat Boy. He sat at the corner thinking that he was just tripping, but he waited until a stream of cars to come down 601 and pulled out in front of them and sped towards the city. Before he could get to the light at the intersection of 601 and Chestnut he noticed that the Impala was coming up from behind. He thought that he wasn't tripping and something wasn't right. He had his turn signal to turn right because he was going to put the 75 grand in the storage and get a few more bricks to sell, when he saw that the Impala had the right turn signal on also. When the light turned green, Ali turned his signal off and drove thru the intersection but not to his surprise the Impala turned his signal off also. As soon as both cars made it thru the intersection the Impala lights and sirens came on. Ali knew that he was hit.

After being pulled over, a few other cruisers pulled up. Even thou he had about 10 cars, Ali never had a driver's license. So when they discovered that, he was asked to get out of the car and when he was being put in the back of a police car he heard one officer say "Look what we got here"

Orangeburg Calhoun Detention Center

It had been 2hrs and Ali was still sitting in the holding cell with no charges. His mind went to thinking about the storage unit key that he had, and knew it was over 50 bricks left and that it would sink in for life. It was no way the local narcs could know about the storage unit unless they had been following him the last couple of weeks. He was also thinking about the money he got caught with and how he was going to explain that. Before long he was taken over to the Sheriff office where he was led to a conference room with several narcs and detectives were sitting around the money stacked table.

"So Mr. Haggard, where did you get all this money from?" one narc said

"I'm a club promoter, I do shows"

"Get the fuck outta here, this drug money" another narc said

"I don't sell drugs"

"Where your guns at? You not scared to ride with type of money on you"

"What I need guns for, I'm not doing nothing illegal"

"So when did you change professions, you don't rob no more" a detective asked. He had arrested Ali on a few arm robberies from back in the days.

Ali laughed and shook his head. Then the head Narc agent Teddy Hogan spoke up. "Ali, you have 3 options here,' Option 1 you sign over this money to the Orangeburg Sheriff office,' Option 2 you claim this money and fight to get it back but we still keep it,' Option 3 You don't know who money this is and we found it." Everybody sat in silence for about 5 minutes. "So what it's going to be" Agent Hogan asked

"What you mean?" Ali asked

"This money"

"What money"

"The money we found in your car"

"I don't know what money you talking about"

"Well all you have to do is sign this paper"

"I ain't signing no paper so you can come back and lock up"

"No son, if you sign this paper that states this is not your money and you don't know anything about this money, we can't lock you up for it."

Ali read the paper and saw what he need to see so he signed it. With that done, he was released with no charges, but was 75 grand short.

December 2007

It was Christmas time and Ali was in good spirits. He felt as if he was Santa Clause and he was playing the role very good. After Tyler gave birth to his Baby Girl in October, he now had 7 kids by 6 different women. He still stuck to his motto "Ali loves the kids" and was going all out for his rug rats. After taking a little break after getting caught with the money, he finished selling the bricks and gave Miquel all his money. He still felt like leaving the game was a good move but what he didn't plan on or think about was all the bills he had. Ali sat and calculated up his monthly bills and it was well over 10 grand a month. He had car insurance for about 10 cars, 3 households that he paid all the bills, daycare for 7 kids was just a few bills that he had and that's not including his shopping and club habits. It seemed like every week he was taking out a 10-stack bundle. He knew that he was going to have to do something to offset the money he was spending.

Chapter 37
"Feels Good To Be Here" Shawty Lo

February 2008
New Orleans, LA All Star Weekend

"Can I get a size 3 in that outfit, size 7 in that outfit and size 10 in that outfit" Ali tells the girl helping him pick out clothes.

"I know that you are shopping for you girl, but I don't think she will be able to fit all these different sizes"

"Naw, it's for 3 different ones, I like them in all shapes and sizes" Ali smiles and looks her up and down.

"Player Player, Huh"

"I tell you what, you pick out an outfit and let me see how you look in it and I will buy it for you". That was all that needed to be said. She went and picked out a Christian Audiger outfit and worked the dressing area like a runway. After spending over 2 grand and exchanging number Ali left the store and headed towards Bourbon Street. "Yo, where you at" he asks thru the cell phone.

"I'm down here in front of this seafood store" Ricky responded. This All-Star weekend was no different from any other. Ricky and Ali was in the city to show out. Well there was one difference, Ricky brought his wifey along but they were still shopping and hitting all the best restaurants as always. He didn't know if Rickey could turn up that night but he had him a New Orleans chick to entertain him if need be.

Chapter 38
"Feel it in the Air" Beenie Siegel

2 weeks later

"Early bird gets the worm" Ricky says thru the cellphone

"What they do homie" Ali answers groggily

"Get your ass up and get to work"

"Alright, I'm about to get up"

"You taking that retirement shit too far, I aint retired so I'm chasing this paper"

"I got you player, I'm getting up now"

"So what you going to do"

"I got like 3 strippers at the house but they about to leave as soon as I touch-down" Ali said in code. Ricky knew the code and they conducted business.

"How many bitches do you want to come to the party today, my cousin coming thru with some bad bitches" Ricky said

"If they bad, I want 10 bitches but I want them too young to drink but I want them to act grown when they get in the swimming pool" Ali responded

"Man, these hoes look like they 26 or 27 when they get wet"

"Alright, I'm going to hit you as soon as I get down there" Ali said. They both would talk in code when they talked about drugs. Ali told Ricky that he had 3 bricks left but they were already sold when he got to Orangeburg. Ricky asked Ali how many bricks did he want because the connect was on the way. Ali wanted 10 bricks but he wanted some good work that would cook up. Ricky confirmed that each ounce was coming back to 26 to 27 grams.

Meanwhile @ Orangeburg Sheriff Department

"We have information that Adrian Haggard will be in town today with a large amount of drugs." The head narcotic agent says in the briefing of the day.

"About how much drugs should he have?" Officer Color asks

"Between 3 to 10 kilos"

"Damn, he is going to have that much on him"

"That or the money to buy the drugs"

"So what are we supposed to be doing"

"That's a good question because we have no clue to where his stash house is located or where he sells the drugs at so we have to find him" Officer Teddy Hogan says

"How we going to do that" another officer asks

"By pulling every car over that he drives" Officer Color says and pulls up a projection screen with all the known cars that Ali drives. They had pictures of all his cars.

"Do you think that he will be driving with all those drugs in those cars" An officer asks skeptical

"Let's not forget that I pulled him over and he had 75 grand on him and he was driving the 650 BMW and that the most expensive car up here" Officer Hogan says and wraps up the meeting. "And remember, he does not have a driver's license."

Dash Street

Ali was inside of the Thomas brother's mobile home counting the money from 2 kilos he sold to one of his customers from Dixianna. "Yo Malcom, you still got that big scale I left here a long time ago?" Ali asks

"Yeah Big Homie, why what's up?"

"I need to break this brick down"

"I thought you don't break down no more?"

"I don't, I got something that I need to do' I got T-Nasty from St. Matthews that want 3 Mike Vick's (three quarters of the kilo), and my partner Nook just got out and I'm going to throw him a big 8"

Doing quick math, Malcom came up with a good question. "So, what you going to do with the other Big 8".

"I'm going to let you do what it do" Ali laughed because he knew that's what Malcom wanted to hear.

After he finished breaking the brick down, Nook pulled up with some chick he was fucking. Ali went outside and gave him the Big and they chopped it up for a few. Nook let him know that he was going on the block and that he would get at him when he finished.

About 2 hours later, Ali was still at the Thomas brothers house waiting on T-Nasty when he got a call from Nook. He was bored and wanted to chill with Ali for a little bit. Once he made it over to the spot, Ali was about to go to the gas station to meet T-Nasty. "Jump in, I'm about to see somebody real quick". When they got to the Lil Cricket gas station on 601, Nook went in to pay for the gas while T-Nasty and Ali did business. By the time Nook came out the store, T-Nasty was pulling off.

Making a right onto 601, Ali spotted an unmarked police truck on the opposite side of the highway. As they passed the unmark, Ali could see the truck brake lights activated and then the truck made a U-Turn in the middle of the highway. "SHIT" Ali said out loud.

"What's up" Nook asked

"That's the fucking police behind us, hold this right here" Ali says as he passed Nook about 9 grand cash.

"What you about to do?"

"I'm about to pull over"

"Dawg, you can't do that, I just got out of jail"

"You straight, that aint 10 grand"

"Man, I got dope on me"

"Cuff that shit, put it in your ass or something" Ali said thinking Nook had a little bit of weed on him.

"I can't put all this in my ass" Nook said pulling the Big 8 out that was still in a big rock form.

Ali had a decision to make. Should he pull over and risk losing about 20 grand more to the Orangeburg Sheriff dept., or should he make sure his partner that just came home after doing time for drugs didn't go back to jail. Ali thought it is what it is. "My nigga listen, I'm going to turn down Jamison and punch it, when we get a good distance, I'm going to stop and jump out, make sure you take that shit with you, don't leave that shit in the truck."

"Alright, good looking"

After jumping out of the truck, Ali ran towards Colman Ave to this chick house he knew and Nook ran towards Ashley Ave. Ali wasn't concerned about the Infiniti truck, he was puzzled about the reason why he was pulled over in the first place. He decided to call this girl named Mya he was fucking, who brother was a police officer. Once he got off the phone with her, he knew that he had some changes to make. Mya had information that let Ali know that things were getting hectic in the city. Not only did they know all the cars Ali drove, they knew he when he was coming to town and how many bricks he was supposed to have. It was some shit in the game and Ali had to get ghost for a minute. He knew that he had to get out of South Carolina so he went in the stash and gave Shakira 50 grand to put a down payment on a house in Charlotte, North Carolina.

Chapter 39
"Fallin" Jay-Z

Ali was sitting at an outside table at the Cheesecake Factory located in South Park mall. Shakira had purchased a house within walking distance. He was feeling good and comfortable now that he was in a bigger city. With the Charlotte Hornets and Carolina Panthers players around, his cars didn't stick out anymore and that was a peace of mind in itself.

"Damn, this how you doing it" Ricky ask as he sit down.

"It feels good to be here, all that money you got, you need to leave the Burg also" Ali quips back

"Fuck that shit you talking, what you know good"

"It's a drought but all I got to do is make a call"

"I'm trying to get 5 of them" Ricky said. Ali went to thinking about Black Biker's Week in Myrtle Beach was coming up and he wanted to have some fun. He knew the kind of fun he was going to need a few grand to blow.

"You aint fucking with Bike Week this year?"

"Naw, mi. going down to Miami, to say you move from South Carolina, you stay down there" Ricky says

"You know I love the city, I got rich down there, so for bike week you know I got to put down for my city" Ali said with a smile

"Get your shopping carts, bricks on isle 9" Ali said quoting one of Gucci Mane lyrics

"You know I got a flight to catch tonight, what time you coming thru?"

"I'm going to stop by the house in the metro and then I'm on the way"

"Don't take too long, I got some shit I need to do"

"You know I got you". Ali said. He just copped 10 bricks from the Cubans and had sales for all of them. Money was going to meet him in Columbia and get 4 of them, Ricky was going to get 5 of them and Lil Blue wanted the last one. He knew he was going to have about 10 grand to blow for the weekend.

While traveling down I-26 he was trying to think who daughter he was going to put his dick in down at Bike Week. While in thought, he didn't notice the dark colored SUV behind him about 3 cars back. He was on the phone with this chick who he named Pretty Pussy because that's what she had and he forgot to tell his driver to get off on exit 139. He told Malcom to get off on the next exit. Fuck it he thought, he would come into the city off the interstate. As they were approaching exit 145 he noticed an Orangeburg Sheriff cruiser on the side of the interstate. He knew that was strange for them because the interstate was Highway Patrol and State Trooper territory. As they passed the cruiser Ali swore he saw the same narc that pulled him over and confiscated the 75 grand. That bothered him but what spooked him was when they passed the patrol car pulled out in traffic behind them. Ali started to panic and told Malcom to switch lanes and when he did, the cruiser switched lanes with them. They passed exit 145 and when they made it to the next exit Ali could see that it was a State Trooper on the incoming ramp so he told Malcom to keep going. Ali knew something wasn't right and when he looked in the rearview mirror he saw the blue lights come on, he made to the quick decision to make a run for it. "Pull over on the side and let me jump out". He reached in the back seat and grabbed the Prada bag and put it on his back. When the car pulled over, he jumped out and ran into the woods. As he got into the woods about 20 yards he threw the Prada bag down because the 6 bricks were weighing him down. After running about 5 minutes, out of breath and out of shape, the police had him surrounded. "FUCK!!" was all he could say.

2 weeks later

Ali was sitting in his living room thinking about what all went wrong. He just took a major loss and had some new state charges for trafficking cocaine. After making the half a million dollar bond, 50 grand cash, and the 6 bricks he just got and not to mention they found a safety deposit box key and found an additional 50 grand cash, he was taking hit after hit. He just got back from retaining one of the best lawyers in South Carolina, Jerry Finney and that was another 25 grand just for the down payment. He was in deep thought about the feds picking up the case because of the amount of drugs he was caught with, they were sure to come. Drinking Grey Goose straight out of the bottle did nothing to brighten his mood. His cell phone started ringing and he looked down to see it was Ricky calling. Ricky just like the rest of his loyal customers was still fucking with him. Even after getting busted and out on a ransom they still needed work and knew that he could produce. He just wasn't in the mood to make the moves. "What they do playboy?" Ali says as he answers the phone.

"Nothing much, just seeing what you up too?"

"In here trying to get drunk but I can't"

"What they lawyer talking about?"

"It's still too early for anything"

"Why you bonded out on that half a million dollar bond, don't you think the feds going to come for that"

"I think they going to come anyway, I had 6 bricks left"

"So, you spent 50 bands and they going to lock you back up and give you another bond?"

"I aint tripping on that, I have over 100 stacks out on the streets that I have to get. You know how it is when a nigga get locked up, niggas get ghost or amnesia when they owe you money" Ali let Ricky know why he wanted to get out.

"So, what's up? You aint trying to make that money back" Ricky asked him

"My head spinning so bad, I don't know if I'm coming or going"

"I'm trying to get right and spend some money, so if you hear anything, holla at your boy"

"I got you, I might do something next week"

The next day Ali was standing in his living room looking out of the window just thinking of a song on one of the rapper Lil Boosie mix tapes "The feds on the way". He knew they was coming and could sense it. After about 10 minutes, he saw what he could feel. Unmark cars were coming in from all directions. He picked up his cellphone and called O-Zone.

"Yo Yo" O-Zone answered

"They here to get me"

"WHO"

"THE ALPHABET BOYS". After a brief silence, he put the phone down and walked outside because he knew it was over with.

GAME OVER!!

Epilogue

After thinking about and replaying the movie of his life in his head, Ali was more than ready to respond and answer the question. "Top, I look at it like this, I never like being without, I never liked being broke. That's my biggest fear ever." He explained to Top about the pros and cons of what he saw in the game. Yeah, he was away doing time but at the same time he couldn't see himself being broke and miserable. He thought about all the fun he had and all the different places he went and knew for sure he would not have been able to do that working a regular job. Ali wasn't an ordinary nigga and what he did, ordinary could not get you.

"I love my kids and family and I hate being away from them, but I lived a good life"!!!!!!

CPSIA information can be obtained
at www.ICGtesting.com
Printed in the USA
BVHW03s1407290518
517632BV00013B/181/P